BUSKIN'
WITH
H.
ALLEN
SMITH

Other books by H. Allen Smith

BUSKIN' with H. Allen Smith

TRIDENT PRESS
NEW YORK

This book is gratefully dedicated to Beck, Sheehan Bryan, Fowler and Blair, who comprise the high-principled Watch & Ward Committee of

THE BROTHERHOOD

CONTENTS

BUSKIN' IN A SALOON WITH SAWDUST ON THE FLOOR

So, my good friends, brim up your cups and load your flagons anew and we'll be ready for this first session of buskin'. It might be wise if I got things started with a brief analysis of the word itself. There is no connection between the verb *buskin'* as we employ it here and the noun *buskin* as designating a high laced shoe affected by the actors in Greek and Roman tragedies.

To *busk,* says the great British word-man Eric Partridge, is to peddle obscene songs and books in public houses. A *busker,* in Mr. Partridge's definition, is the vendor of such merchandise or, more properly, a man who sings or recites in a public house.

In his fine fat history of vaudeville the late Joe Laurie, Jr., told us that buskin' was a common pursuit all over the United States back in Civil War times. Professional entertainers went buskin' to get eatin'-money or, more probably, drinkin'-dough. They might have been singers, or dancers, or jugglers, or players upon the swynet, but more often than not they were raconteurs, storytellers, monologists. They went into the saloons or the pool rooms or the lodge halls or the whorehouses and did their routines for "throw money." Mr. Laurie reports that the sharper ones among them sometimes hired shills to begin tossing a few coins, a process known in higher economic realms as pump-priming.

I hasten to assure you that I am not one of the sharper ones; I have hired no coin-tossers. I'm after the folding stuff.

9

Joe Laurie, Jr., thinks that the buskers of yore may have been the people who originated vaudeville. The practice of buskin' for "throw money" became so widespread that hordes of fireside show-offs and parlor smart alecs took to roaming over the country-side, performing in taverns and cathouses and back of the tents at the county fair; then along came a wise guy who decided to wrap up some of this itinerant talent into one big package and put it on a stage and charge admission. There is something stimulating in this picture until we arrive at the depressing fact that the end result was Ed Sullivan.

And so it is, my friends, that you find me settled in your midst this evening, buskin' in the good old-fashioned way. My qualifications? Well, a good memory, for one. If I set myself to it, I can re-member dozens and dozens of stories and anecdotes, and many of them score well in company. I have been listening to stories all my life, beginning with behind-the-barn sniggerings in the Mid-dle West, moving on to side-of-the-mouth narratives in the pool halls of my native heath, and reaching full flower in the culture-heavy city rooms of a dozen newspapers in the North, the South, the West and the East; and more especially, in the drinking dives around the corner from those newspapers.

▪   ▪

But I was speaking of my memory. The other day I paid a courtesy call on my doctor and he requested that I define my ailments.

"Nothing wrong," I said, "but the slow, steady disintegration of the meat."

I didn't bother to tell him that as I fumble-mumble my way into the sere-and-yellow years, I grow more forgetful. I lose things. God how I lose things! I have to make notes to remind me of things that I need quite desperately to remember, and I lose the notes. I sit around with friends who occupy my age-bracket and we indulge in warm discussions of The Golden Years, and curse them roundly, and vie with one another telling tales about our desiccated memory-knots. I confess that my own knot grows tighter and is steadily dwindling in size until I feel sure it is no bigger than a mouse doodle. Yet within that doodle I seem to have retained the stories, or at least a lot of them. And the one that usually makes a hit with people who are themselves losing their memories concerns the man who, so afflicted, presented himself before a psychiatrist and said: "Doc, I'm in bad trouble. I can't remember anything."

"Anything?" repeated the psychiatrist.

"I mean everything," said the patient. "I cannot remember a single damn thing any more."

"You mean, of course, such things as names and faces and maybe dates."

"I mean *every* thing!"

"Oh, that's ridiculous," said the doctor. "It's not possible. It has never happened to any human being in history."

The patient said: "I'm telling you, Doc, I can't remember *anything*. Everything I see, everything I hear, everything I read . . . it all just funnels through my head and vanishes forever. That's the truth, Doc. I simply cannot remember one . . . single . . . God . . . damn . . . thing!"

The psychiatrist frowned, and bent his head and gave the matter some study, and then he said: "How long has this been going on?"

"How long has *what* been going on?"

■   ■

Please, Madam, don't throw money yet.

It might be fitting at this point, folks, to interpolate a tale of the theater, since we are indulging tonight in a sort of theatrical proceeding. This story is told about several towns in the early West but I heard it Phoenix and since I am running this show, and since I am an authority on life in the Untamed West . . . Phoenix by God it stays.

In the time when Phoenix was the metropolis of Arizona Territory one of those traveling theatrical troupes arrived and set up a tent and began presenting a series of plays.

One of their melodramas had a rather spectacular beginning. The curtain rose on a bedroom scene. Asleep in the bed was a

11

young woman, a beauty. Into the room stepped the young woman's husband. He strode to the foot of the bed, glared down at the sleeping girl, pulled out a pistol, leveled it at her and then shot her. Realizing the enormity of his deed, he now let the pistol fall from his trembling fingers, staggered backward aghast, clapped a hand to his forehead and cried out in anguish: "Good God what have I done!"

On the day this dramaturgical tidbit was scheduled for presentation the girl who normally played the part of the wife (she was actually the wife of the stage manager) took sick or ran off with a Goldwater or some such thing. So now the company manager told the stage manager to go downtown and scout around the streets and find a local girl to play the part. "Tell her it's worth five dollars," he said, "and explain to her that she doesn't have to speak a single word, doesn't have to do a damn thing but lie still in the bed and get shot."

The stage manager soon located a striking blonde who was willing to pick up the five and so that evening when the curtain rose on Act I she was in the bed, eyes closed, a sweet smile on her lips. Into the room came the impetuous husband. Up to the bed. Bang! He staggered back and clasped his brow and cried out, "Good God what have I done!"

Out in the audience a whiskery geezer leaped to his feet and yelled back:

"Ah'll tell ya what ya done, ya son of a bitch! Ya just killed the best God damn whore in Maricopa County!"

Yes, things are looking up. As of today it is not only possible to tell a good salty Catholic story in the presence of Catholics; it is possible to tell it without saying first, "This one I got from a Catholic friend of mine." This condition applies, in varying degree, with all creeds, races, political parties, labor unions, service clubs, nudist colonies, and Boy Scout troops. Matters are loosening up. The only real dangerous ground remaining is that occupied by the quivering boobs who believe in ectoplasm, flying

12

saucersful of humanoids, ESP, astrology and the half-baked drool-ings of that hallucinated woman in Washington, D. C.

Notwithstanding this exhilarating collapse of civilization, I find myself growing just a trifle nervous in the telling of certain types of stories. I know quite a few Catholic stories but right now I think I'll move in gently. This one is about two little boys who were proceeding along the street when they encountered Father Boyle, who was walking in a painful bent-over posture.

"My goodness, Father Boyle," exclaimed one little boy, "what happened to you?"

Said the priest: "I fell off the commode and hurt my back."

The boys expressed their sympathy and then walked on, and pretty soon one said:

"What's a commode?"

And the other replied: "How should I know? I ain't Cath'lic."

■   ■

Or this one, just brought in a day or so ago by my staff Catholic:

A young priest, understandably excited at the prospect of de-livering his first sermon, asked an older priest to be present and observe his performance.

When it was over the young priest hurried to the older one and asked eagerly, "How did I do?"

"Quite excellent," said the veteran, "except for a few misstate-ments of fact, which I am sure were simply the result of inex-perience."

"Like what, Father?"

"Well, there are ten commandments, not fifteen. Jonah did not swallow the whale. And there is not going to be a Peter Pull at Saint Taffy's on Thursday night."

■   ■

George Bernard Shaw, who was surely one of the ablest and most highly cultivated of men in human history, once said: "The ablest and most highly cultivated people continually discuss religion, politics, and sex: it is hardly an exaggeration to say that they discuss nothing else with fully awakened interest." I ride shotgun with Shaw.

An unmarried lady in a Maryland town arrived at her 100th birthday and a reporter called on her and asked her the usual questions.

"Have you ever been seriously ill?" he wanted to know.

"Never," she said.

"Haven't you ever been bedridden?"

"Twice," she said, "and once in a buggy."

■　■

Brotherly love can be a many-splendored thing, especially in the Carolinas. I remember an evening I spent with a substantial citizen of North Carolina, a Tar Heel of some importance on the political scene as well as in the business world and a man who usually wouldn't say shuckin's if he had a mouthful. This gentleman and I were enjoying some corn-squeezin's, which agreed with him to the extent of making him maudlin about his brother P. J.

"In those days," said my important friend, "I didn't have a great deal of reliance in myself, especially in matters of major concern, and I always made a practice of getting my brother's opinion on my problems.

"The time had come for me to think of getting married and being a person given to indecision, I was courting two stunning girls at the same time. One of them lived in nearby South Carolina and the other lived in the North Carolina town where P. J. and I lived. At that time a marriage license cost two dollars in North Carolina and three dollars in South Carolina.

"Now, I want you to know that I loved each of those girls with equal passion and fervor and yearning, but I realized that I could save one dollar by marrying the girl in North Carolina. It was a big decision for me to make so as usual I took my problem to P. J. I secretly hoped that, because of the economic factor, he would favor the girl in North Carolina, and I hinted that that was what I wanted, but he wouldn't go along. I pressed him for a decision, telling him *how desperately* I needed his help, and finally he said:

" 'Well, Tom, if you really insist, I must tell you that I've screwed them both and in my humble opinion there's not a dollar's difference between the two.' "

Glasses filled? Hit the gargle a little more heartily, friends! Nobody ever told a good earthy story over a glass of milk. Old Pythagoras once observed that a man is not considered to be thoroughly drunk until, lying flat on the floor, he spreads out his arms and legs to keep himself from dropping any lower.

Back where I come from it is said that one of the town characters was found at dawn lying unconscious in the middle of the street. A crowd soon gathered and finally someone said: "Hell, he ain't drunk. I just seen his finger move."

All of you appear to be upright and alert. Hold the pose while I relate the story Bob Burns used to tell about his uncle, the one with the scientific approach. Uncle Fud, I think his name was.

Uncle Fud went up on a mountain back of Van Buren and found a huge rock poised at the crest. He worked with planks and fence rails for hours and finally dislodged the monster and it went bounding down the mountainside.

It headed straight for the town and behind it, running hard, was Uncle Fud. The big boulder crashed through the livery stable, shot down the main street, went through the First National Bank and finally came to rest against a tree in the rear of that institution. The townspeople were gathering from every side when Uncle Fud arrived on the run. He shoved everyone aside and approached the rock, which he scrutinized carefully through a magnifying glass. Finally he straightened up and said:

"Nope. No moss."

A single afternoon with W. C. Fields at his big house on De Mille Drive was sufficient for a fat chapter in one of my early books. I remember his saying that he had a happy childhood. When he was a boy in Philadelphia he worked as a helper on an ice wagon. His job was to carry the smaller chunks from the wagon to the customer's icebox. "Got twenny-fi' cents uh weeeeeek," he said, "and all th' ice I could eat."

I have taken note of the happy boyhood enjoyed by several other comics.

"The first time I ever saw a woman," said Cliff Arquette, "I was fifteen years old. I thought it was a smooth sheep."

Joey Bishop has mentioned his childhood in connection with a discussion of parental discipline. "I was whipped so much," said Joey, "that till I was twelve I thought I was a dog team."

In similar vein Richard Pryor has reported that the principal of his school in the Midwest whipped the boys with a large wooden paddle. "The wood had holes bored in it," he recalled, "and he hit you hard so your meat come through the holes."

Echoing the carefree boyhood of Cliff Arquette, another comic whose name escapes me has remarked: "Till I was twelve years old I thought a girl was a soft boy."

■　　■

David Lilienthal tells of two old gents sitting on a bench in front of the courthouse.

"Eph," says one, "you recollect in years past how we useta set on this bench and watch all them purty girls goin' by in their springtime dresses?"

"Yep. I remember."

"You remember how we useta look at their purty bottoms when they walked by?"

"Yep. I recollect it. What I *can't* remember is why."

■　　■

One afternoon I was watching Art Linkletter interviewing the little kids on his television show. This day he was asking them to tell their favorite stories out of the Bible and then to tell the lesson they learned from those stories.

One little boy chose David and Goliath. He told it quite well and with fair accuracy and when he was finished Linkletter asked: "Now, what did you learn from that story?"

The boy said: "Dodge rocks or you'll get your head knocked off."

■   ■

Long years ago one of the top contenders for the heavyweight boxing title was an amiable roughneck named Tom Sharkey. At one period in his career he was training for a bout with James J. Jeffries. Sharkey favored a conditioning regimen of drinking great quantities of beer and eating as much food as he could hold. He spent a lot of time around a certain saloon where the beer was good and the free lunch more than adequate.

Gene Fowler used to tell about how Sharkey put such a dent in the saloon's buffet that the owner of the place had to do something about it. Sharkey was a public figure, widely admired, and so the problem had to be settled with a certain finesse. One day the proprietor said to his bartender:

"Take away all this free lunch for a couple of days. Then get some dog biscuit. The hardest God damn dog biscuit there is. If you can crack it with an axe, we don't want it. What I mean is, we want real *hard* dog biscuit. Then let's see if this Sharkey son of a bitch can go on eating us out of house and home."

The dog biscuit was installed where the pickles and sausages and hams and turkeys had been. Following his workout, Sharkey arrived at the saloon and saw the biscuits and sampled one, then proceeded to eat his way through the whole concrete pile. The next day he did the same, amid great smacking of his lips. So now the saloon owner said to the bartender:

"It's no use, Al. Clean up the crumbs and put back the regular lunch. That son of a bitch Sharkey!"

On the third day, then, Sharkey arrived and cast an eye over the hams and pickles and sausages and so on. He seemed a trifle confused. Then he turned and called out to the bartender:

"Hey, you, where in hell's them *tasties* I been havin' lately?"

■   ■

A few years back Nunnally Johnson, the talented screenwriter, observed to a friend that he had been married three times, and had a set of children by each of his wives. The first brood was grown and had children of their own; the second batch were in their twenties and beginning to produce young, while the third group consisted now of adolescents.

"I believe," said Mr. Johnson, "that I'm the only man in the United States who has been reading *Little Black Sambo* out loud steadily for thirty-five years."

■   ■

There was a time when Ed Sheehan's radio program originated in a tree-house studio perched in a giant banyan at the International Market Place in Waikiki. Ed did his disk-jockey show from this shack forty feet above the ground for quite a few years. When Don Quinn inspected the setup, his comment was:

"If you wanted to work in a crotch why the hell didn't you become a gynecologist?"

■   ■

Some of you may have heard of The Brotherhood. Six of us make up the total membership. Two are in California, one in New York, one in Hawaii, one in Virginia and one in Mexico. There are a few associate members. The bond that holds us together is a sort of round-robin correspondence by which we exchange wholesome thoughts, and advise one another of our individual adventures, and narrate inspirational stories and anecdotes that have come our way. We all happen to be on the same wavelength, so far as humor is concerned, and the Brotherhood has but one requirement to make of its members: make it funny or get your ass out.

It is my intention to conclude each session of this seminar with a *Recitation*, the kind of high-minded declamation we used to have at grade-school graduation exercises, a tender valedictory, so to speak. A few of these will be lifted from the archives of The Brotherhood. If some should have a familiar ring to you, please keep in mind that the Copying Machines are loose upon the land, and some of our papers have had a contraband circulation approaching that of Corey Ford's classic, *How to Guess Your Age*.

I note that a few of you are getting slightly stoned, so let us polish off this first evening with . . .

RECITATION NO. 1

Medical Memo to The Brotherhood:

In case anybody has been wondering where I have been lately, this is to report that yesterday I emerged from the hocking fusspital.

Transurethral resection for benign prostatic hyperthropy. Benign my ass. What they did was they rammed some kind of a periscope, of the type used to look at parades when there are a lot of other idiot parade-watchers jammed up in front of you . . . they rammed this here periscope clean up and all the way through my whammadoodle . . . and some distance beyond, I suspect.

The object they were after, as I get the golden word, was a thing the size of a Land Rover snow tire—a mean antisocial son of a bitch that had wrapped itself around the neck of my bladder, and then started tightening in like a boa constrictor. This made it all but impossible for me to piss—a procedural verb which, under medical law, doctors are forbidden to speak, saying instead, "void." The nurses also called it void. They'd come into the room and say, "Did you void yet this morning, Mr. Smith?" These were nurses to whom I had been telling a whole series of dirty stories from time to time, with huge success—stories with words in them that constricted the adhesive tape on patients three doors down the hall. So I would reply to the nurses, "If you mean did I piss yet this morning, well I . . ." By this time they would have flung up their hands in shock and fled from the room. There is no understanding women.

Now, let me say that I had the best pecrologist in all of Westchester County, a man I have known socially for several years. I was keenly interested in the style and flair for which he is famous in this line of work, and I wanted to watch, but the bastard had me put to sleep and I never saw any of the action.

I *still* don't see how he swung it. He had that periscope rammed up yonder, with all kinds of optional equipment fastened to it and dangling out of it. So he had to lean down between my legs and close one eye and sight into the view-finder (I am reconstructing this account of the invasion through pure theory). He had to sight into it, as I say . . . he had to look up there quite a distance. About a foot and a half, I should say. God damn it, don't interrupt! After he spotted what he was looking for, he probably hollered, "Double rear-view mirror with slasher and tongs, nineteen swabs, and prepare for a possible explosion of void!" So they handed him this special instrument. I didn't see it. I don't think I ever *want* to see it. It had to be poked up inside that steel tunnel (my God what my Thing must have looked like at this point!). I assume that it had a little air-cooled electric bulb on the upper end, to illuminate the scene of action. Then there would have to be a little slanted mirror on *his* end of it—he couldn't keep his eye fastened to the end of my diddledywhacker as if it were a telescope, else he wouldn't have been able to manipulate that back-geared lathe. Obviously he couldn't reach all the way in there with his left hand and grab things and hold them still while cutting on them. For this one seeming fact, at least, I am grateful.

Somewhere alongside that little light at the far end was a knife, or a patented apple-parer big enough and sharp enough to cut little chunks away from that prostatic snow tire and, in addition, a pair of tiny ice tongs to take hold of the meat chunks and drag them down the corridor and out into God's clean air. I don't know what he did with them after he got them hauled out. I feel sure he didn't save them. They'd have made good chili.

Anyway, I am now at home, filled with plenty of void but very little vinegar. It was all quite enlivening and I have no criticism to make of anybody, except maybe a small general quibble against the doctors. I wish they would improve their penmanship and think up a livelier way of saying stool.

ANECDOTES
THAT AMUSE THE RICH

Brander Matthews wrote a famous essay, *On the Antiquity of Jests,* covering his subject quite adequately. André Maurois told of the woman who, in 1880, was reading *The Life of Jesus,* and who begged of her friend, "Please don't tell me what the end is like." Forty-five years later, said M. Maurois, a woman was attending the play *Saint Joan* and said to her friends, "Don't give away the ending." I can add a dovetail incident that occurred twenty years after that when Toots Shor was taken to see a Broadway production of *Hamlet.* At the end of the first act Shor told his pals in the lobby, "One thing for sure, I'm the only one here who don't know how it comes out."

The jests repeat themselves year after year, decade after decade, century after century. I do not intend to steer away from jokes during these sessions but a sensible course, I think, would be to lean heavily on the anecdote as against the jest. An anecdote is usually a biographical bit with a punchline, a story about a real person, and I have run up against several million of them in my time. Quite often they have, at least, the semblance of originality.

I spoke earlier of my years in the newspaper business. I worked on country weeklies and on metropolitan dailies and I met some fabulous creatures within The Second Oldest Profession. A quip comes to mind—a lady society editor of a New York paper, accustomed to traffic among Astors and Vanderbilts, once unbent in a downtown saloon with a few of us and said: "This business we're in is like an old, old dose of clap to which one ultimately becomes accustomed and even a little attached."

I reach casually into the ragbag of memory and come up with Jimmie Larkin, who was once a warm friend and who has been dead now a dozen years. Drink. Peritonitis brought on by long years of hard boozing. Yet Jimmie had a happy life and a large part of his happiness could be traced straight to Clarence Darrow's testicles. I rarely think any more of Jimmie Larkin; I was involved personally in the event that shaped his future, and somehow it never occurred to me until this very hour that the story of Jimmie and Darrow needs to be told.

Jimmie came out of Buffalo and, I think, was a clear misfit in the newspaper business (as so many others are). He was a desk man, lacking the special knack that makes a reporter. Circumstances would arise, however, and Jimmie would be sent out to cover a story—usually one of no great consequence. One evening in the 1930s I had a date to interview Clarence Darrow who was to speak at a banquet in the Hotel Astor. Somebody murdered somebody else out on Long Island and I got stuck on that story, and the boss pulled Jimmie Larkin off the desk and sent him to see Darrow. Later that night Jimmie told me what happened:

When Mr. Darrow opened the door to his room my God there he stood in his old-fashioned B. V. D.'s. He was about eighty years old and looked it. But nice. I mean nice. He was just as nice to me as if he had known me all my life. His balls were hangin' out of the front of his underwear and I want to tell you I never saw the like of it—God Almighty they were hangin' halfway down to his knees. He didn't even seem to notice it. So here we were, and I asked him a couple questions about the speech and he sorta mumbled the answers and all the time he was startin' to put on a stiff shirt, and after he got it on and fumbled around with the studs and dropped them on the floor and I had to find them and pick them up for him, and then I put a couple of them in where he couldn't find the holes. So then he gets out a bow tie that had to be tied, and got it around his neck, and messed with it and grumbled and swore a little. He asked me if I could tie a bow tie. He says, "Mrs. Darrow usually does this for me." So I tackled it, and thought to myself, "Good God, look at me, tyin' a bow tie right on the great Clarence Darrow! I'll remember this all my life!" And so I finally got the God damn thing tied right and then . . . I tell you, Allen, you won't believe this . . . he looked down at his balls and mumbled something and I looked at them, and I swallowed hard a couple of times and thought, "Sheeez! Clarence Darrow's balls! Halfway to his knees!" So he reached down and took hold of them with his right hand and held his shorts open with his left hand and eased them up and sorta poured them back inside. They dropped right down, seems like a foot below the leg of the underwear, which didn't look right, but he says, "That'll do 'er." And then he says, "Mrs. Darrow generally does *that* for me, too." I helped him a little, getting into his pants and so on, and he kept thanking me, and says that if he tried to do all that by himself he'd be so worn out he wouldn't be able to make it to the speakers' table.

That's about the way he told it to me. When he finished there was a long thoughtful pause. I couldn't think of any appropriate remarks and after a while Jimmie just shook his head, as if to say that the impossible had occurred, and he murmured: "Clarence Darrow's balls! In person!" He wrote no story. He didn't have one.

■   ■

For a while after that I would see him sometimes sitting at his desk staring straight ahead, a dreamy look on his face, and I could almost tell that he was thinking of Clarence Darrow. He quit telling other people about the incident because they usually laughed. He knew quite well that there was a comical side to it, but it was much more than that—it was, for him, a real close brush with fame. He somehow felt that for a rare moment or two he had been closer to Clarence Darrow than anyone else had ever been, except perhaps Mrs. Darrow.

A few months later Jimmie was fired. He went into publicity work for a while, and then vanished, and I heard once that he had been drafted into the army in World War II. Then one day I came face to face with him on the street in Beverly Hills. He was sober and looked trim and healthy, though his clothes were on the seedy side. We went to a tavern and sat down for a couple of hours and talked about earlier adventures together and I asked him: "Jimmie, do you remember the night you subbed for me and almost got to play Ping Pong with Clarence Darrow's balls?"

"I've never forgotten it," he said, and smiled. "That was a crazy thing, I know, but it did something for me—I had never had any contact before with a real famous man, and you couldn't get much more famous than Mr. Darrow was. I know it's crazy the way it sounds, but *it wasn't a bit crazy when it happened.*"

He said he had been busted out of the army as an alcoholic and had been a beach-bum for several years but then he got hold of himself and married a nice girl who was a nurse. At the moment Jimmie was clerking in a Thrifty drugstore and he said that he didn't get drunk except about once every two or three months. He had no thought of returning to the newspaper business. He knew he wasn't cut out for it, and he was quite happy the way things stood. He said he had two hobbies. He grew flowers around the little house where he and his wife lived. And he was a collector. He collected every book he could find—every shred of writing that was concerned in any way with the life of Clarence Darrow.

Well, wouldn't you?

■ ■

The kooky citizens of the States that border on California hold themselves far superior to the kooks of California itself. It is possible for the inland kooks to be pleasant to kooks who arrive among them in automobiles with California license plates, but they are nonetheless contemptuous. It is their firm belief that Californians have fewer brains than God gave geese.

My old friend Fred Beck, who was once a newspaperman himself, used to divide his year between a beach house in Malibu (where a street was named for him) and a house in Ketchum, Idaho. The Beck car always wore California license plates.

Matt Weinstock has written that Idahoans "generally are suspicious of invaders with California license plates. They've heard awful tales about us and some visitors from Los Angeles manage to tarnish our already smudged reputation as a boorish lot, spoiled by success and luxury."

Fred Beck got off to a shaky start in Ketchum by using worms to catch fish. This set him apart from the town's star fisherfolk (including one Ernest Hemingway) who were philosophers and fished with flies. Artificial flies. Mr. Beck was not totally condemned for worm fishing, but the practice put him under suspicion, and the bank wanted a lot of collateral out of him.

There came a time when he decided to build a cabin for use as his study and a man with a bulldozer arrived to clear and smooth down the site. On this particular day Mr. Beck decided he would have a try for some trout and he went out to gather bait. On impulse he asked the bulldozer man to run his machine over a certain spot where he usually found a lot of worms, and the bulldozer man did it, and there were fishin' worms all over the place, and Mr. Beck gathered them in his can.

Next day, down in the town, Mr. Beck found himself being pointed out and regarded with new interest by the natives.

"That's him," they'd say. "That's the fella from California not only fishes with worms, but uses a bulldozer to dig his bait."

Mr. Beck was never able to live it down and so, in time, rather than skulk through the back alleys of Ketchum, he moved away to a place he calls Cat City in the California desert. In Cat City he is sometimes regarded as strange. Not for his piscatorial techniques, but for various other idiosyncrasies. I hope to take up a few of them in a later seminar.

■　　■

Harry Truman was making a speech at a Grange convention in Kansas City. Mrs. Truman and one of her friends were in the audience. Mr. Truman told the husbandmen that the key to success in farming was wrapped up in one word. "Manure," said Mr. Truman, "Manure, manure, manure, manure, and more manure."

Down in the auditorium Mrs. Truman's friend whispered behind her hand: "Listen, Bess, when are you *ever* going to get Harry to say *fertilizer?*" Replied Mrs. Truman: "Good Lord, Marge, it's taken me thirty years to get him to say *manure!*"

■　■

A dozen years ago in Charleston, West Virginia, there was a man who owned a small business which had grown so prosperous that he was able to sell out for $70,000. To him this was an immense sum of money and he decided to take his wife on a trip to California.

They stopped off at Las Vegas to have a look. He watched the play at the tables for a while and then joined in the fun. Within a few hours he was stone broke, penniless. He went to the men's room and discovered he needed a dime to get into the booth and he didn't even have the dime. He borrowed one from a stranger and insisted on getting the man's name and address so he could mail it to him.

Returning to the booth he discovered that the last occupant had left the door slightly ajar and the dime wasn't needed. On his way back to the lobby he dropped the dime into a slot machine and hit the jackpot. He took the money back to the crap game and when he finally walked away from the table he had well over a hundred thousand dollars.

Arriving home in Charleston he happened to remark to his wife that he had incurred a debt that he would never be able to repay.

"I thought," said his wife, "that you mailed the dime back to the man who gave it to you in the toilet."

"Yes," he said, "I did, but the true and immediate cause of my good fortune in Las Vegas was the man who left the door to the toilet open, and I'll never know who he was."

■　■

A lot of people think that the expression "a gone coon" has a racial connotation. Not so. The origin is zoological, according to the evidence of the books.

In Vermont a long time back there was a captain in the United States Army named Martin Scott, who was celebrated as a sharpshooter. He was so expert with his rifle that his fame was known all over the Eastern part of the country.

Captain Scott was out for a stroll one morning, carrying his gun, when he spotted a raccoon perched high up in a tree. He raised his gun to his shoulder, whereupon the animal held up a paw as a signal for a parley.

"Excuse me," said the raccoon, "but would your name, by any chance, be Scott?"

"It is," said the Captain.

"*Martin* Scott?"

"That's right."

"*Captain* Martin Scott?" persisted the animal.

"Yes. I'm Captain Martin Scott."

"Well, then, I'm a gone coon."

■　■

Little Bobby's parents bought him a parakeet and the boy promptly developed an inordinate affection for the bird. He hated to leave for school each morning and in the afternoons he rushed straight home to play with his pet.

Arriving home one day he found his beloved parakeet lying dead on the bottom of his cage, his little feet sticking straight up. The boy went into hysterics. He shrieked and screeched and kicked and flopped around on the floor and his mother could not get him calmed down, so she telephoned her husband and urged him to hurry home.

Bobby was still howling and raging against Bitter Fate when his father arrived. "Come now, Bobby," said his father, "let's sit down and talk about this." He took the boy in his arms and sat down and then began discussing the tragedy in a soothing voice.

"I'll tell you," he said, "what we'll do. I'll go down in the basement and make a pretty little coffin that will just fit Chirpy. We'll wrap him up in some white silk and put him in the coffin and tack the lid on. Then we'll go out there in the back yard and dig a little grave alongside the forsythia, and I'll fix up a nice headstone for him, with his name and the date on it, and *your* name too. Then we'll give him a wonderful funeral."

By this time no more than an occasional sob was coming from Bobby, and he was paying close attention.

"This will be," went on his father, "the best funeral any parakeet ever had. You can invite all your friends—ten, twelve, fifteen, twenty if you want. We'll take the phonograph out there and have some soft music, and if you want to do it, *you* can speak a tribute to Chirpy, deliver what they call the eulogy, and say whatever you want to about him. Then he'll be buried, and after that . . . well, I tell you what. All of your friends will stay right here, and we'll have what they call a wake. There'll be all the ice cream that anybody can eat, five different flavors, and half a dozen different kinds of cake, and a bag of candy for every kid present, also a little gift for each one, and in addition to that . . ."

A slight noise was heard in the room and they turned toward it. Chirpy the parakeet was back on his feet, eyes wide open, shaking himself. Father and son jumped up and crossed the room and stared at the resurrected bird. They stood there speechless, one long minute, and then Bobby spoke: "Let's kill 'im!"

■   ■

This hardware guy came back from a convention in San Francisco and was telling his friend about a girl he had seen performing in a night club.

"This gal," he said, "has a fifty-four inch bosom. She doesn't have any talent but she's got a real good act. All she does is crawl out on the stage, on her hands and knees, and then try to get up."

■ ■

A newspaper friend in New Jersey has written me about the Palisades Park elephant doodles. The park is across the Hudson from New York City, occupying a site high on the cliffs that are known as the Palisades.

A couple of years ago one of the star attractions was an act consisting of three elephants. After the show each evening the two handlers had the job of cleaning up and they took the easy course, sweeping the litter over the edge of the cliff.

Nestled at the bottom of the cliff is the town of Edgewater, and one evening the Board of Adjustment was in session. Into the room came a distraught homeowner and without a by-your-leave began telling, in anguished tones, of a terrible happening at his residence.

"We were entertaining some friends on the patio," said the householder, "and along about the second martini, down from the sky came great thundering elephant turds, big as basketballs gentlemen, plummeting all over the lawn and the terrace and one of the ladies was hit right square on the head by one of those immense turds that broke into a million shreds, and that lady is still in bed with a nervous breakdown."

The Board of Adjustment could do nothing, except to speak sharply to the management of the amusement park. The warning was couched in legalistic terms, foreseeing all contingencies, forbidding the sweeping of any "elephant residue" over the cliffs in the future, or "any residue of any kind whatsoever."

■ ■

A related story (related only in the commodity involved) concerns one Jimmie Finch, a veteran employee of the circus, whose job was to follow along behind the procession of ten elephants as it circled the big tent, using his little cart and broom to clean up the leavings.

One night Jimmie arrived home in a rage and stomped around the house, muttering and yelling curses, and when his wife could get him calmed down he told her that the circus management was bringing in *eighteen more* elephants and adding them to the procession, so that now he would have to clean up after *twenty-eight,* because they were refusing to put on extra help.

"Well," said Mrs. Finch, "I don't blame you one bit for being sore. Listen, Jimmie. We've got a nice piece of money put away and you're not getting any younger, and you don't have to put up with this kind of treatment. Why don't you just march down there in the morning and quit?"

"What?" exclaimed Jimmie, his eyes bugging out. "And give up show biz?"

■   ■

Which in turn brings up a little story told by Harry Hershfield, about the elevator operator in the old *Journal* building on South Street in New York. This man worked for six or seven years at his job and then suddenly vanished. A couple of years passed and one afternoon Hershfield ran into him in a saloon near Park Row.

"What happened?" he demanded. "Where'd you disappear to?"
The man stared glumly into his beer and then said:
"The newspaper game's all shot to hell."

■   ■

Jennie was getting married and the moment had come for her mother to give her the Big Confidential Talk.

"Darling," she said, "I think I have one real good piece of advice for you. Never undress completely in front of your husband. Never! Always keep at least one article of clothing on. It's much sexier that way."

A month or two later Jennie's husband decided that his moment had come for a Big Confidential.

"Tell me something, Jennie," he said, "is there any history of insanity in your family?"

"No, of course not," said Jennie. "Why on earth do you ask?"

"Oh, I don't know," said her husband. "It's just that since we're married you've never once taken off your hat."

■ ■

A man of many accomplishments and a man I greatly admire is John Kenneth Galbraith. A few years ago he did a book about his growing up in Ontario. It was a most pleasant book, titled *The Scotch*, and in it I found this story:

At some time during adolescence, I encountered a novel by Anatole France which made unlicensed sexual transactions, especially if blessed by deep affection and profound mutual understanding, seem much more defensible than I had previously been allowed to suppose. It was summer and I was deeply in love. One day the object of my love, a compact golden-haired girl who lived on Willey's Sideroad, a half mile away, came over to visit my sisters. They were away and we walked together through the orchard and climbed onto a rail fence which overlooked a small field between our place and Bert McCallum's. Our cows were pasturing on the second-growth clover in front of us. The hot summer afternoon lay quiet all around.

With the cows was a bull named O. A. C. Pride, for the Ontario Agricultural College where my father had bid him in at an auction. As we perched there the bull served his purpose by serving a heifer which was in season.

Noticing that my companion was watching with evident interest and with some sense of my own courage, I said: "I think it would be fun to do that."

She replied: "Well, it's your cow."

■ ■

The local dramatic group was putting on a play in what might have been called their Theatre in the Round in the Woods. The stage was a cleared spot at the edge of a forest and the audience sat on campstools.

In the audience was a young man who had brought his girl friend to the play, which had something to do with the exploits of Robin Hood. The young man had been belting away at a flask before the proceedings. Along toward the end of the first act he excused himself, left his girl, and went to the rear where he asked an usher to direct him to the men's room.

The usher told him to walk left until he came to an oak tree and then go left again about twenty paces. The boy departed and finally arrived back at his seat.

"Has Act Two started yet?" he asked his girl.

"You oughta know," she said. "You were the star in it."

■　　■

Colonel Lemuel Q. Stoopnagle, of fond memory, once advanced the brash opinion that parades are not properly organized. Each person on the sidelines may have a particular section of a parade he wants to look at longer than the other sections—perhaps he has a friend or a relative in that section, or he may be the man who designed the costumes or made the flags or decorated the floats. The section he particularly wants to see goes past him before he has a chance to take it all in and if he wants to study it further, he has to sort of trot alongside it. The Colonel proposed that all future parades be formed up along a stretch of Fifth Avenue, or whatever street being paraded, and that the marchers and floats and bands and twirlers and horsemen and cops and everybody else in the parade stand still, so the onlookers could walk around them and take a leisurely look at the sections they happened to like best.

■　　■

Now I would like to tell you a brief tale of a Swede who came to this country a while back and got a job in a small factory somewhere in Ohio. He was a pecunious Swede and after a few years of earnest labor he had saved enough for a vacation back in Skövde. His folks and friends all wanted to know, of course, what the Americans were really like. He said they were very nice and friendly people but that they were not altogether like Swedes and in some matters had strange and mysterious ways.

"You take," he said, "the fellas in my shop I work with. There is one who is near seven feet tall and they call him 'Shorty.' There is one who is bald, no hair on his head, and they call him 'Curley.'

There is one who weighs better than three hundred pounds, and they speak of him as 'Half-Pint.' And me—me, a fella who has not been with a woman in fifteen years—they always refer to me as 'that fuckin' Swede.' "

■　■

We are all acquainted, I think, with the occasional literary tidbit that got into circulation in former times through the medium of the mimeograph machine. Today such small popular classics are spread to the winds by the monster Xerox and all its relatives. Some of the items in this category might best be called set-pieces, but I think we can handle them under our general head of "Recitations." Now and then they get published in odd places and if they happen to be wholesome and sanitary, a few have made it in the folklore collections.

Thus we arrive without much pain, I hope, at the hour for . . .

RECITATION NO. 2

December 31, 19——.

Dear Pal:

Well, here it is, the end of another year, and as is my custom I take out a little time to write a few of my good friends—it is the time when I remember all the good things that have happened to me in the past twelvemonth, when I reflect on the value of the friendships I have cherished over the years, when, in fact, I indulge myself to the extent of waxing a bit sentimental.

It's a snowy evening, the doorbell rings intermittently, but here in my den it is cozy and comfortable and peaceful. I'm sitting before a nice open fire with my typewriter, sort of half-listening to the hi-fi, and slowly sipping a nice very dry double Martini. I surely wish you were here but since you are not, the least I can do is toast your health and happiness for the coming year, so time out, old pal, while I bend my elbow with thoughts of you.

I just took a recess to mix another Martini and while I was out in the kitchen I thought of all the time I would waste during the evening, chasing back and forth, so I just made up a big pitcher of martinies and broughggt it back in with me so I'd have it right here beside me and wouldn't have to wast time making more of them. So now I'm all set and here goes pal. Besides Marinis are a great drink. For some reason they nevr seem to have the effecr on me in the slightest that they have on oter fellas. Can drinj them all day longg so here goes.

The greatest think in tje whole word is friendship. A n believe me pal you are the greatet pal anybody every had. do you rember all the swel; times we had to gether pal/ The wonferful times on the road 1811 never forgt the time we were in Tledo and met that babe in the swlloon that redhesd. You rascl you. I remenber you kept puting brandey in my drinj whehn I wasennt looking and it made me sicj and you rascale you snuck ofd with the redheed brod. Ha. ha. Boy hoew we laughd dint't we. It was pretty funny anywah. I still laught abot it onec in whiel. Not as mcuch as usd to. But whag the hell after all you stilk my bedst old pal pal. And if a guy canot havr a laughg with a treu froe, md once in a wihle waht the fuxk.

Escue me. Pictcher was empt so I just mde nother one. hot dam. I sure wish yoi were her olf pal help me drinj thes Martuni because they arw simptly delidious. I lifty my glasx to you good health oncemore you are the bests pall I got. Of cours why a pal would do a dirrty thing like that load up a pals drinj with branidy mak him sick as a dof, lousyt thing for antbody to do, onlhy a firdt class prock wold do a thing lije that. Wasnet a bit funny and if yoi thinj its funnyu you are aboyt the worsr dhit heeel I evre had the midforyune to make the aquantentce of you sonb of birfh lous and as far as O am concerbed yot can go to helk and on th way kisa my ass.

STORIES TO
FRACTURE PEOPLE AT FIRES

Bob Hope once spoke feelingly of a gentleman who had gone to college and majored in Nasty. It is my impression that Mr. Hope was not favorable toward the gentleman. Be that as it may, I would like to announce that if some college wants to use this collection of lectures as a course of study, it is all right with me. It will liven up the gray matter of the young people and send them forth into greater trouble than they are already in. Any school that wants the lectures will have to pay for them, the reason for my mercenary attitude being that I just plain enjoy the gelt.

At the same time I would like to make it known that I am not at all shocked by the moral depravity of today's young people. Things could be worse.

My wife served time as a teen-ager in a small Missouri town during the corrupt and prurient period that followed the first World War. This was the time when mothers kept an extra supply of soap around for washing out the mouths of vulgar-talking children.

One evening in the 1920s my future wife was indulging in a household rite known as arnin. Idly she began to sing the key line from a popular song of the period: "Sit down, sit down, you're rockin' the boat." Her father, a stern man, rose from his rockin' chair, gave forth a great bellow of indignation, and ordered:

"Don't you ever let me hear you singin' that song again in this house as long as you live!"

"Why, Papa?" asked Little Nelle.

"It's nasty dirty, that's why!" he said, and it may be worth noting that from that day to this she has never stood up in a boat.

During this same era my sister Lou lived in Washington, D. C., and our younger brother Sam was a boarder in her home. Sam had a talent for using hard language on occasion and Sister Lou disapproved, often warning him to mind his dirty tongue. One day he cracked his ankle against a heavy chair, which of course had no business being there in the first place, whereupon he assembled the nine parts of speech into a series of highly colorful and smoking clauses.

Sister Lou now issued an ultimatum. Any more of that kind of talk and Sam could find himself another place to live. He crossed his heart and hoped to die.

A few evenings later he came in from a date and with no thought of offending anyone, *he* sang the key line of a popular song: "But last night, on the back porch, I loved her best of all."

"Pack!" ordered Lou. "Out!" she proclaimed, pointing to the door. And into the snow and sleet he went.

Just recently, on a spring day in the year 1967, I was walking along a public thoroughfare in New York City and I heard a teen-age girl brazenly chanting the key line from a popular song, as follows: "Doo-waddy-dee-diddy-did, whoo-whee-waddy-wad." I blushed. Then I reached into my pocket, but I had left my bar of soap at home. I had an impulse to seize that child by the shoulders and give her a good shaking. And then I realized that this was exactly the way *we* behaved back in the time of our tenderness. Whee-waddy-wad-diddy-do and quit rockin' the boat!

■ ■

The dirty-talkin' town of Alvarado, where I sometimes visit, is on the Gulf coast of Mexico, a short drive south from Veracruz. It is a community with a unique reputation and once in Veracruz my friend Carlos Campo explained:

"Alvarado is famous because the people curse more than anywhere else in the world, even the women and children. They cannot speak one sentence without including one or two curse words, and some of them very bad, very dirty words. It is their ordinary way of talking, and they do not think there is anything bad about it."

I asked Carlos if he could give me an example of the way the Alvarado people talk and he said that well, maybe two or three men or women would be standing on the street and they say goodbye and one of them might add, "*Adios,* and say hello to your son of a bitch mother." Something on that order, or worse, said Carlos.

He then told of the Bishop of Alvarado, who had grown up in the town, and who decided the time had come to preach a sermon against cursing. "You must learn," he told his parishioners, "to control your temper, you must not get angry at little things, and then you will not use such bad language all the time. Now, right at this moment, there is an innocent little fly on my hand. I can feel him walking around. I know that most of you would curse him if he were walking around on *your* hand. But he is only a little fly and he will do me no harm and he will go away and anyway he is one of God's creatures, so why should I curse him?"

At this point the Bishop glanced benignly down at his hand, and then exclaimed: "God Almighty! The son of a bitch is a bee!"

■　　■

Some years ago I returned to the town in Southern Illinois where I was born and in the course of my rambling around I met a middle-aged woman who was famous locally for her piety. She was the wife of a well-to-do businessman and she was militant against drinking, smoking, cussing, gambling, and other pleasant things. One day she told me a story—such a story as I would never permit within the pages of a book bearing my name, except for the incredible fact that it came from the lips of such a devout and dedicated person. We happened to meet down at the courthouse square and were standing and talking when the subject of our conversation sent me off on a story which I realized, too late, was slightly off-color. I had to go on with it and I did, and arrived at the risqué punchline. I wouldn't have been at all surprised if that lady had turned her back on me but, instead, she tittered, and then she asked me if I ever knew Ferd Clemming. I said I hadn't.

"Ferd," she said, "was a fellow worked as a clerk in the hardware store here. He was a little short and skinny man, baldheaded and very bashful. One day there was a trashy peroxide blonde came to town. I can't remember what she came here for but, anyway, she walked into the hardware store and Ferd Clemming waited on her. She said she wanted a doorknob and Ferd went and got it for her and laid it down on the counter in front of her. Then he looked at her and said, 'You wanna screw for this doorknob?' And that peroxide blonde said, 'It's all right with me if it's all right with you.'"

I swan, you never know what to expect in McLeansboro, Illinois!

■   ■

One of the characters around New York in the pre-television 1930s was an old bag from Brooklyn named Sadie Hertz. Sadie spent all her spare time attending audience-participation shows in the various studios of the radio networks. She was often called upon to answer questions in the quiz shows because her responses were sometimes entertaining.

One evening I heard the man ask her, "Name some great events that occurred between 1860 and 1870." Sadie mulled this one over for half a minute and then delivered.

"Turrible things," she said. "They had a centennial. Things was turrible. McKinley and Buchanan and Lincoln was all killed. It was a turrible centennial."

Another time the Shakespearian line was tossed at her: "Good night, good night! parting is such sweet sorrow, That I shall say good night till it be morrow."

"Now, Sadie," said the man, "just what precisely did Juliet mean when she said that line to Romeo?"

"Recite it out again," said Sadie. He repeated it.

"Now," he asked her, "what was she saying to Romeo?"

"G'night," answered Sadie, "see ya tuhmarr."

■　■

Along about that same time Ed Gardner, the star of "Duffy's Tavern" and a very funny man, attended a production of *Hamlet* at a Broadway theater. That is, he was in his seat when the curtain went up on Act One.

At intermission a newspaperman in the audience ducked out and scurried to a bar across the street for a quick one. There stood Ed Gardner, a large highball in front of him.

"Did you leave in the middle of the act?" the newspaperman asked.

"Yeh."

"How come?"

Gardner drew himself up and with great hauteur said:

"Shakespeare should always be spoke slow."

■　■

An English huntsman was making his way through the gorse and bracken and other stuff they've got over there, and he came to a clearing where a beautiful young woman was standing, wearing very little in the way of clothing.

"I beg your pardon," stammered the hunter, grown all fidgety with embarrassment. "I'm looking for game."

The girl smiled and said, "I'm game."

So he shot her.

■　■

Mr. Woltman, the journalist, was driving home from work and about half a dozen blocks from his house he spied little Susie Kantor skipping along the sidewalk in the direction of her home. The Kantors lived next door to the Woltmans, so Mr. Woltman stopped and asked Susie if she'd like a ride home. She said she would and climbed in and they started off. Almost immediately Susie asked Mr. Woltman if he'd mind stopping at the filling station which was on the way home, and he said he wouldn't mind at all, but would she tell him why? She said she had to go to the baffroom.

"But Susie," said Mr. Woltman, "you'll practically be at your own house when we get to the filling station. Can't you wait just two minutes till you get home?"

"I could," said Susie, "but I don't wanna, because *we're* not sanitized."

■   ■

Not long ago I heard about the doting mother of a professional football star who always watched the games on television and cringed whenever she heard the sportscasters call her boy an offensive end. "Oh," she'd complain, "I wish they wouldn't call him that—he's not a *bit* offensive."

Makes me think of the old farmer who was brought in town to the hospital, bad sick, and he heard his nurse say to another nurse in the corridor outside: "He's quite critical." When the nurse came back into his room he protested. "I'm not a bit critical," he said. "I think ever'thing's jest fine!"

■   ■

Herman Hickman, the hefty football coach who came out of the Shallow South, was a great storyteller. I remember the time he was telling about a hunting trip in the Tennessee mountains. He and three Nashville businessmen had been climbing around in the hills all morning and at last they came to a little grocery store stuck off in the woods and run by an old hillbilly guy right out of the classical mould.

The huntsmen were having some sandwiches and one of them began to speculate about the weather prospects for the remainder of the day and the old storekeeper spoke up.

"Ah was just up to muh cabin," he said, "and Ah heard the man on the radio say it was gonna rain this afternoon."

"Oh, well," said the hunter, "in that case I think we'd better just turn around right now and head back for the place where we left the car."

"Now, jist a minute!" spoke up the hillbilly. "Don't you pay any mind to what I jist tole you. It's only a cheap little ole radio."

■　　■

Sam Rogers, a character in a novel I wrote a while back, sends me a story about a fellow from Middle Europe who arrived penniless in the United States ten years ago and settled in a small midwestern city.

After a few years of unobtrusive living, this man suddenly bought one of the fine houses in the town, and he began to show other signs of prosperity. The fact of his moving into the grand house impressed the president of the local Rotary club, and he prevailed upon the man to come to a Rotary meeting.

At the meeting the club president spoke glowingly of the immigrant's achievements, emphasizing that this was another instance of the great opportunities awaiting a man with energy and determination and foresight in our great nation, and then he asked the guest to get up and say a few words.

The Mittel European, in broken English, told about his arrival in the town with a dime in his pocket. He took the dime and bought shoelaces and sold them for twenty cents, and then bought more shoelaces at a dime per pair, and continued selling them at twenty cents, and at last he had saved enough to send for his brother in the old country. Now there were two of them selling shoelaces, and business was good, and . . . he paused to take a sip of water and the Rotary president broke in with: "And from this humble beginning you have gone forward in the American tradition, working hard and saving, and now you . . ."

"No, no," said the humble one. "My brudda and me we just keep sell shoelace till we have enough money to bring over our sisters and open up whorehouse."

■　　■

When I first told this story, nigh onto thirty years back, I didn't reveal the name of the protagonist. It was Jimmy Cannon, then a Broadway columnist and later one of the nation's top sportswriters.

Jimmy was a young and vigorous chronicler of the doings of show-biz people. He'd turn in his copy at night and the next day it would appear with copy-desk alterations and deletions. He soon grew waspish over the manner in which his column was being butchered. He found out that a certain lobster-trick copyreader, a man past sixty, was responsible, and one night he telephoned this copyreader.

"Mr. Doyle," he said, "I don't want you to get sore now but I'm damned well fed up with the way you've been trimming my stuff."

Mr. Doyle held his peace.

"After all," went on Jimmy, "this is Broadway I'm writing about. You don't know anything about Broadway. You never get around the hot spots. You're not qualified to pass on Broadway topics. Now, admit it, Mr. Doyle."

Mr. Doyle took his time. At last he said:

"Yes, Jimmy. You're right. I'm just a country boy. I don't know a thing about Broadway and the night spots. I never been in one of those night clubs. I don't see Times Square once a year. I'm a country boy, brought up on the farm, spent all my life on a farm, got my education on a farm, and there's only one thing I know. I know horse shit when I see it."

■　　■

In 1942 when H. L. Mencken published his *A New Dictionary of Quotations* I was mildly surprised to find in its pages items of this calibre:

Jump
Yeesus, what a yump!
> Exclamation of a legendary Swedish-American who made a wild leap to board a steamship that was leaving its pier, landed on his head, and on recovering consciousness and looking back found that he was half a mile from shore.

When I get around to doing My Very Own Book of Quotations it is my intention to include remarks of a similar quality, and things like the following:

"I was a shy kid. I wouldn't take a bath till they blindfolded my rubber duck."

Jackie Vernon.

"You're not really poor till you start using water on the corn flakes."

Mrs. David Markson, wife of an author.

"She who never tooteth her own horn, never gets tooteth."

A mother's advice to Debbie Reynolds.

"The lightning flashed, the thunder roared, and brought forth a chigger."

Alben W. Barkley, speaking of certain events in Republican Washington.

"I have a compulsion to return to the womb. Any womb."

Woody Allen.

"After we eat this apple we're gonna do *what?*"

Adam (to Eve).

"We are living in the Millennium of the Mental Midget."

David Susskind.

"Go to the grocery store and get ten cents cockroach powder but don't tell them what we want it for."

Sam Levinson's Mama.

"The three ages of man are: Youth, Middle Age, and You're Looking Good."

Cardinal Spellman & Others.

"He'd be all right if he took his finger out of his mouth."

Harold Robbins, of Truman Capote.

■   ■

A rather hard-bitten broad with a paid-up membership in the Jet Set (sometimes called The Beautiful People) awoke in her New York apartment at noontime, feeling incredibly fierce. She groaned a few groans and then whimpered and as she came more awake she had a feeling that something was wrong with her hair. She put a hand up and felt around in the hair and came away with some grains of rice. She tried to think, tried to remember, but nothing came clear. Then, in a tone of almost total resignation, she said:

"Well, I either got married again last night, or I got puked on by a Chinaman."

■　■

Here come those two old maids again. They had a fine sow and kept her in a pen at the back of their property and one day the vet told them that the time had come for them to have her bred. He said the animal should be taken to Mr. Miller's place, a quarter of a mile up the road, where there was a boar of ample attainments. The old sow was quite enormous and refused to walk any distance at all, and so the maiden ladies managed to get her into a wheelbarrow and up to Mr. Miller's. The next day they took her again and on the third day hauled her up the road for her final processing. On the fourth day when the old maids got up and went out back, there was their sow, already in the wheelbarrow, ready to go.

■　■

In the days of the whaling ships Captain Peleg Hawes was saying goodbye to his wife Arathusy; the moment had come again for him to depart on a cruise that might take two or three years. Arathusy wept some, as was her custom, and then she begged:

"Oh, Peleg, 'twouldn't be so hard if you'd only write me a letter while you're away on these eternal long v'yages! You never write me one single letter. Promise me, Peleg, this time—just *one* nice letter from way off yander!"

Captain Peleg Hawes didn't hold with such frivolity, but he grumbled out a promise. Eighteen months later the letter arrived at the Hawes house. It read:

■   ■

Toward the end of his life John Barrymore was on tour in a dog of a play and in Chicago his leading lady took sick. Another actress was flown in from New York to try for the part. She met with Barrymore and the play's director in Barrymore's suite at the Blackstone.

After a brief discussion about the play itself, Barrymore began making broad gestures and indulging in alarming facial contortions and assorted body jerkings, all calculated to suggest to the director that he wanted to be alone with this girl.

So the director said he had an errand to perform and took his departure. He walked along the hotel corridor and made a turn toward the elevators and came to a small window that opened into the Barrymore suite. An inspiration came to him.

"All my life," he said to himself, "I've been hearing about The Great Lover. What a kick to see him in action! How I'd love to know his technique!"

He gave the corridor window a gentle push and it swung open. Through a doorway he could see Barrymore, still in the same chair and staring across at the actress, who was not in view. Barrymore was wearing his demoniacal Rasputin face. He was not talking— he was simply leering as nobody ever leered before.

The director leaned forward, his eyes on Barrymore, his ears attuned. Then it came. In a deep-throated voice Barrymore suddenly spoke. Said The Great Lover:

"Hey, kid. I'd like to hump you."

RECITATION NO. 3

José Maniah was a cook in a Southwestern cow camp. To all appearances he was a lowly paisano yet beneath that rude exterior was the soul of a poet and the heart of a lion.

A cowboy had the misfortune to cheat José Maniah in a game of cards whereupon José killed the man dead. A jury swiftly found him guilty and José was brought before a certain Judge Isaac Parker, a man who believed that Mexican blood was evil blood and the less of it in the world the better. Said Judge Parker:

José Maniah, stand up! You have been found guilty of a most heinous crime. As a usual thing it is a painful duty when a Judge must pronounce upon a human being the sentence of death. There is something horrible about it, and the mind of the court naturally rebels at the performance of such a duty. Happily, however, your case is relieved of all such unpleasant features and the Court takes positive pleasure in sentencing you to death.

Soon it will be springtime and down in the wild and beautiful valleys will be heard the bellowing of the frisky bull and the artless prattle of little children as they come home from school. But you won't hear any of it, José Maniah, because you will not be present. Nature will be putting on her gorgeous robes, and the birds will be singing their sweet carols to the sky, but you won't see any of these things, José Maniah, because you will not be here.

The flowers will not bloom for you, José Maniah. The birds will not sing their carols for you. And after happy summer, then comes the dreary winter, but don't let that cause you any anxiety, José, for you won't be here.

It is customary, at a time such as this, to invoke the tender mercies of a Higher Court. But if I thought God Almighty would have any compassion for a wretch such as you, I would never think or speak of Him again—you cold-blooded, chili-eating, saddle-colored, pepper-bellied, sheep-herding son of a bitch you.

José Maniah, I gladly and eagerly and with happiness swelling in my heart order that on the sixth day of the coming month you be hanged by the neck until you are dead, dead, dead. Take the son of a bitch away.

That might have been all, had the sheriff yanked José Maniah out of the courtroom at once. But José Maniah had words to utter. He faced Judge Parker, and this is what he said:

That I have taken human life I do not deny, but it was under circumstances of the greatest provocation. So determined was this Court to add another to its long list of slaughtered victims that I early foresaw my doom was sealed. You have sat here through the proceedings of this hellish farce with a ghoulish glee portrayed on your every feature. You and your bloodthirsty jury remind me more of a lot of buzzards hovering over an expected victim, than of a body of men supposed to guard and honor the principles of human justice. Hear me, you half-starved hyena! You cannot break *my* spirit!

You speak of the pleasant odor of blossoms and the sweet singing of the birds, you grandson of a pock-marked whore. You announce to the world that I am to be hanged. As I gaze on your bloated, whisky-fogged face I find no surprise at your satanic conduct. With mock solemnity and cruel sarcasm you have consigned me to an ignominious death. Very well, you disheveled barbarian, you wild-eyed, dirty-nosed, pot-gutted, carnivorous offspring of a cross-eyed maggot—I want you to understand that your words hold no terror for me.

You tell me that on the sixth day of the coming month I am to be taken out and hanged by the neck until I am dead, dead, dead. You hope in your filthy heart that my corpse is left dangling until the vultures come down and pick my bones clean. You do not even have the grace to call down the mercy of God on my soul.

And I, José Maniah, I say to you that on the sixth day of the coming month I will *not* be forever deprived of the sweet sounds and the pleasant odors of which you have spoken. As for hanging by the neck until I am dead, dead, dead—you can kiss my ass until it's red, red, red, and may God blast your dirty old soul!

That is the end of it, save for the legend that José Maniah broke jail a couple of days later, escaped into the hills, and was never recaptured.

FAIRY TALES
THAT FAIRIES LIKE

A woman I have known for two dozen years, a mother of four, a vigorous worker for civic affairs and charity, a lover of music and painting and literature, stopped by my house a few days ago for a long visit on the terrace. I told her that the day might not be far off when she would disavow her friendship with me, for I was working on a collection of stories and jokes and anecdotes, and that a good many of them would be bawdy and maybe even a trifle scatological. She astonished me by saying:

"Oh, I think that's a marvelous idea! Hurry and get it finished! And promise me an advance copy."

And then she launched right into a story she said I might be able to use. It was a parrot story and parrot stories are usually just fine, unless they happen to be miserable parrot stories.

This young man bought a handsome parrot and took it to his Manhattan apartment and was pleased with the few comments it had to offer from time to time. Then one evening he brought a young lady home, and they had no more than settled down in the living room when the bird sang out:

"Somebody's gonna get ——ed!" My old friend, who had never in my presence used a word as vile as fanny, or belly-button, in this case used the *awful* word with all of its *hideous* flavor, and I God damn near fell off my chair.

The parrot's declaration was embarrassing to the young man,

and he stammered out some apologetic remarks and got the girl out of the place. The next day he went to the pet store and told the proprietor what had happened.

"Well," said the man, "I didn't make any guarantee about the character of the bird's discourse, evangelical or otherwise."

"I know," said the young man. "It's not that. It's just that I thought if . . . well, my bird is a male, and I thought if I had a female to put in the room with him, that would distract his attention from my own affairs, and . . ."

"I don't have a female parrot in the house," said the storekeeper. "But right over there is a female owl. You think that might work?"

"Let's give it a try," said the young man, and home he went with the owl, and installed her on a perch near the parrot's cage.

That evening the young man arrived with another girl friend, and fixed her a drink, and they sat down.

"Somebody's gonna get ——ed!" the parrot cried.

The owl said: "Whooo?"

And the parrot hollered: "Not you, you flat-faced old son of a bitch!"

■   ■

I was still gasping a little when my circumspect friend gave a yip, and said, "Oh, I just happened to think of another one!" And out it came.

A young man at college in upper Connecticut was ready to drive home to Greenwich for a holiday when a good-looking girl approached and told him she, too, lived in Greenwich, and could she ride along with him.

Off they went and after they had indulged in trifling talk the young man offered the girl a cigarette, and she said she didn't smoke. A while later he produced a pint of Old Happy Stuff and offered it to her, and she smiled and said she didn't drink.

They rode along another half hour and the boy was thinking, what the hell! Nothing ventured, nothing gained!

"Would you like," he said, "to stop at a motel I know about down the line and spend a few hours there?"

"Oh, yes!" the girl cried. "Oh, that would be great! As I always say to the girls in the choir, it's possible to have fun without all that smoking and drinking."

■ ▪

In our own frontier west there were various recipes for coffee, something like this: put the can of water on to boil and add coffee and keep addin' coffee and then add some more till when you throw a horseshoe nail in it will float—then the stuff's ready to drink.

Out in Australia they say that the only proper way to cook a cockatoo is to put the bird into a billy (can) along with an axehead. Boil until the axehead is soft. The cockatoo is then ready to eat.

■ ■

Around the various newspaper shops where I worked in the prime of my life there was usually a man with a collection of typographical errors, known as typos. These composing-room blunders were clipped from assorted newspapers and pasted into a large composition book and the collection grew steadily year after year, affording much merriment around the editorial rooms. I never, incidentally, ever heard of a *printer* who made such a collection. I myself had a collection at one time, but I loaned it to an insufferable etaoin shrdlu prig at the United Press and never got it back.

A collection of typos was almost always one hundred per cent vulgar. The best of them very often were not typographical errors at all, but unintended double entendres. And sometimes a fine effect was achieved through a switching of captions underneath pictures of the same column-width. One of the prizes in my collection was from the old Brooklyn *Eagle*. The paper carried a two-column cut showing a wierd new bird that had just been acquired by the Prospect Park Zoo. On the opposite page was a two-column photo of Brooklyn's leading society woman, wearing the gown she had chosen for an upcoming ball. Beneath the picture of the bird was a description of the dowager and her costume. And under *her* picture were these lines: "Isn't this a strange sort of bird? It has hair where feathers ought to be!"

■   ■

In England a typo is called a "clanger." The most famous clanger, perhaps, was one which appeared in the time of Queen Victoria and in, as I recall, the London *Times*. It was contained in an account of a royal procession, and it was a true typo, resulting in the suppression of that entire edition of the paper. The clanger occurred in the line: "At this point the Queen passed over London bridge."

A few years ago a small book of clangers was published in England by Fritz Spiegl, a musician, and sold like kippers if not trifles. An example of what can happen when a single line of type is dropped out of a story is seen in an account of Jean Shrimpton's costume at a certain function. The Liverpool *Echo* has it thus:

> Lady Nathan said if Miss
> Shrimpton wanted to wear
> skirts four inches above
> her business.
>   "But it is not done here.
> We all took exception to
> her not wearing gloves on
> Saturday."

Also in Mr. Spiegl's little book is the line: "After the dinner Mr. Khrushchev led Mrs. Eisenhower by the arm down the Embassy steps, while President Eisenhower took Mrs. Khrushchev's ars." And in the *Times* Literary Supplement the author of *The Origins of the 2nd World War* may or may not have enjoyed the line: "Here's a provocative contribution from the well-known shitorian." And this bit from a sports page:

> Dead-eye Stewart Fraser, who got three against the league
> of Ireland recently, attempted a shit from 20 yards, but was

so wide of the target that he actually found Carlyle with his attempt. The outside-right was so surprised at the "pass" that he made a mess of his shot at the goal.

■   ■

Mr. Dead-eye Stewart Fraser has had many an American counterpart in the making of messes. The same kind of typo occurred in a cowboy novel issued some years back by one of the nation's leading book publishers. The setting was a tough Western saloon, with our hero standing at the bar, surrounded by blackhearted villains prepared to do him in. At the first treacherous move, the hero went into action. The line should have read: "He shot rapidly three times and three waddies dropped to the floor."

■   ■

A typographical error that gave me pleasure was contained in an account of a bullfight in Mexico City. I am one of those eccentrics who dislike bullfighting and say so in public. Hence my pleasure in reading, in a Mexican newspaper, the line: "At this point the bull turned and snotted at the spectators." I'd have done the same.

■   ■

As mentioned earlier, the double entendre appearing on the printed page is sometimes called a typo. A newspaperman I know in Atlanta once sent me a beaut.

Some years ago the backfield star for the University of Georgia Bulldogs was a guy named Peters. This Mr. Peters took sick or got hurt a few days before the Big Game. The sad news was announced in one of Georgia's leading dailies under an eight-column bannerline, as follows:

BULLDOGS TO PLAY WITHOUT PETERS

The managing editor, when a copy of the paper arrived at his desk, took note of this bannerline and the thought crossed his mind that some readers might detect a double meaning in it. He knew how such things can sometimes stir up the subscribers. He went at once to the sports editor and called his attention to it and suggested that the wording of the line be changed. The sports editor grinned and said that he hadn't even noticed the double entendre before, and that he would make the correction at once. He did. In the next edition the bannerline read:

BULLDOGS TO PLAY WITH PETERS OUT

■ ■

One more. Not long ago I met a lady who was genteel in her manner in spite of having served several years as society editor of a daily newspaper in the Midwest. We got to talking about typos and after considerable hesitation she told me how she had become involved in a splendidly horrible typographical double entendre.

The wedding of the season in this city joined members of two leading families. The bridegroom's name was Cockburn and the Cockburns were rich and also quite proper. The bride, too, was of the quality. It happened that my friend, the society editor, was having a day off when the wedding took place, and an assistant kissed the whole affair off with four or five paragraphs. There were squawks, of course, and on the following day my friend set to work in an effort to correct the mistake. She put a second-day lead on her story and then recounted, at great length, every detail of the wedding itself. This story, too, carried an eight-column bannerline, written by the society editor herself, as follows:

COCKBURNS OFF ON WEDDING TRIP

My friend said she quit the newspaper business a short time later and has no desire to go back to it.

■ ■

A classic tale of an oldtime rural parson in New England has been published by Edwin Valentine Mitchell in his book, *Yankee Folk*.

This Massachusetts preacher had been making parish calls all afternoon and, as was the custom, at each house he was offered a potation of one kind or another, perhaps hard cider, perhaps dandelion wine, perhaps Jamaikey rum. Arriving at the last house on his schedule for the day he got off his horse and dropped the bridle rein over a hitching post.

While the parson was indoors, having another drink or so, the horse got loose, but was caught by a neighbor. The neighbor secured the animal to the post again by passing the rein through the augur hole near the top and then looping it over the post.

When the minister finished his business and came out of the house he didn't seem able to get his horse unhitched. At last the people of the household, noting his difficulties, came out to give him a hand. Retaining as much of his dignity as possible, he gestured toward the top of the post and said:

"Friends, while I was in your house one of the most remarkable miracles ever known took place. My horse has in some manner managed to crawl through the hole in this post, and I cannot persuade him to return."

■　■

It is sometimes said, by misguided Yankees, that Southern towns have more than the national average of feeble-minded people wandering their streets. This is not true. Several years ago I was visiting friends in a town in Unoccupied Florida, up near the Georgia border. They were building a new hospital in this town and, though construction had not yet started, the excavation was almost finished—an immense pit nearly a block long.

It happened that a Mr. Dabney, one of the town's leading citizens, was showing me the site. We were standing by the excavation when a boy about twelve years old came along. He was by reputation the town half-wit; that is, he was *one* of them. He came up alongside of us and stared into the excavation and finally he said, "Mista Dabney, what they gonna do with that big ole hole when they finey git 'er dug?"

Mr. Dabney smiled at the boy and then said, "Well, Hoab, I

tell you. When they git 'er dug they're gonna take all the sonsa-bitches in this town and pile 'em all in there and bury 'em."

The boy reflected on this information a bit and then said, "Who they gonna git to cover 'em up?"

■   ■

A long time ago I attended a luncheon in Atlanta and seated next to me was O. B. Keeler, the town's most celebrated sportswriter. He told me that he had just come from his doctor's office where he had heard a story that was raging around in Atlanta medical circles.

A certain doctor had heard about a new machine which was reputed to be very effective in massaging the prostate gland and because this doctor had a plethora of prostate patients, he ordered one. When it came he unpacked it and found that it consisted of a large flattish box with a hard-rubber "finger" thrust upward from the center, plus a smaller control box with a knob on it. The doctor read the directions carefully and then, like a child with a new toy, grew eager to use it. He stepped down the hall to the office of a dentist, who was one of his prostate patients, and asked him to come over when he could spare a few minutes.

After a while the dentist arrived and the doctor showed him the new machine. The dentist was a bit apprehensive about it, being old-fashioned in some areas, but the doctor finally persuaded him to give it a try. The dentist lowered his galligaskins and got onto the peg and when he was settled there, the doctor carefully turned the knob on the control box until the pointer was on "5."

"Feel anything?" he asked.

"No."

"Stay put," said the doctor, and turned the knob a trifle more, to "10." The directions said that "10" was the recommended setting.

"Feel anything now?"

"Nawp."

The doctor scowled and checked the paper. It said "10."

"You don't feel anything at all?" he asked.

"Not a thing," said the dentist, beginning to grow uneasy.

The doctor took hold of the knob and began slowly turning it, very slowly, keeping a wary eye on his patient—up to "20" and then to "30" and then on to "50" and nothing happened.

"Damn!" said the doctor. "Something wrong somewhere." He glanced around and then suddenly walked over to the wall. "Hell," he said, chuckling, "here's where the trouble is! Thing isn't plugged in."

He picked up the plug and rammed it into the wall socket.

There was a simultaneous loud buzzing sound and a mighty screech from the dentist as he came off the box, his pants down around his ankles. He let go one more scream and his second jump sent him right through the glass door and onto the floor of the hallway.

That ended the sportswriter's story. I didn't ask what else happened. To do so would have been sinful.

■   ■

My old friend Carlos Campo of Mexico was mentioned earlier in connection with the dirty-talkin' town of Alvarado. Carlos can tell good stories by the hour but sometimes he grows a trifle too imaginative. As in the case of the tattooed sailor.

Carlos said that this sailor was a patient in a Mexico City hospital and one day two nurses were talking in a corridor near his room. One nurse was a small plain-jane while the other was more buxom and alluring and, in fact, in the words of Carlos, one hot baby with the big titty. There in the corridor the small nurse whispered to the sexy one that the sailor was tattooed in a most unusual place.

"Where?" asked the voluptuous one.

"On his . . ." said the little nurse, "on his . . . well . . . on his thing. And believe it or not, he has his girl's *name* tattooed on it."

"Oh," murmured the sexy babe with a sigh, "I think that's real cute. But your sailor must be a nut. What's his girl's name?"

"Meda," said the other and spelled it out.

"Meda," repeated the buxom one. "Don't think I ever heard of that name. But this I gotta see." And into the sailor's room she walked. Half an hour or so later she ran into her little friend.

"You were wrong, kid, about that sailor's tattoo," she said. "It isn't his girl's name at all. It says, *Memento of a Visit to Las Vegas, Nevada.*"

After Carlos told this story I suggested that it must have been a Gringo sailor and he grew indignant and said it was a fine up-standing Mexican boy. So I said, well, anyway, I thought the thing had been stretched just a bit too far.

"For maybe *you*," said Carlos. "Not *me!*"

■　■

When I was a rewrite man on the New York *World-Tele-gram* I was occasionally shocked at the ignorance of reporters who were natives of the Great City. Especially as regards the birds and the bees. Particularly, the bees. One afternoon a swarm of bees got loose on Sixth Avenue and congregated on the front window of the Hurley & Daly saloon—the same saloon that they had to build the RCA building around.

Our paper sent a young man to gather a thoroughgoing report on this phenomenon. He was a native New Yorker and here was a thing completely outside his experience. At last he telephoned the office and I got the job of taking the story from him.

"I'm phoning from across the street," he said. "I can see these bastards packed all over the front of the saloon. There must be a couple million of them."

"What's the name of the saloon?" I asked him, for the place had not yet become celebrated as the hangout for two generations of broadcasters.

"Well," said this young Richard Harding Davis, "I can't tell you that. These bees have got the name covered up so I can't read it and I don't want to go over there and ask."

"Why not?" I demanded.

"Hell," he said, "I understand they bite."

■　　■

　　　The rodeo was playing Madison Square Garden in New York and a visiting Texan was wandering around the basement floor of the big building when he came upon an interesting spectacle.

　　　Several men were gathered around a large black bull. One end of a piece of rubber hose, about four feet long, had been thrust into the bull at the rear. And one of the men had his mouth fastened to the other end of the hose and was blowing as hard as he could into it. His cheeks were distended, his eyes bugged out, and the sweat stood on his forehead.

　　　The Texan asked what the procedure was all about, and one of the men told him, "This is a contest called 'Blowing Up the Bull.' The idea is, you pay five dollars, and you blow into the hose, and if you can blow hard enough to make the bull's eyes cross, you win a twenty-five dollar cash prize. You wanta try it?"

　　　Knowing that he had always been possessed of strong lungs, the Texan put up his five bucks and walked to the back end of the bull. He took hold of the hose and pulled it out of the bull and then stuck the other end in. He was about to do his blowing when one of the men said, "Wait a minute, brother. You're not gonna blow on *that* end, are you?"

　　　"I sure as heck am," said the Texan. "You think I'm gonna put my mouth where all you Yankees been puttin' *yours?*"

■　　■

　　　If the State of Texas seems to insinuate itself into these little sessions, it may be for the reason that I have been visiting West of the Pecos a good deal the last few years. Listen to this one.

　　　Tom Jack Woods was "give out to be" the tallest man in Brewster County. He was close to six feet eight, but so skinny that he looked even taller.

　　　Like all men of his size Tom Jack was wearied nigh unto death by remarks of people touching on his altitude. "How's the weather up there?" is a remark that tall people often have to put up with, but in Texas there is a tendency toward more original phrases. "You shore stand mighty high off your corns," is one. And another: "I bet it takes a long time for you to find out when your feet git cold."

One day Tom Jack was in the general store when a traveling salesman in the blue jeans line came in, took one look, and spoke a straightforward comment: "Man, you sure are a tall one."

"Oh, I don't know," said Tom Jack. "I don't consider myself as being out of the ordinary tall. I got a sister that's taller than me."

"A sister? How tall is she?"

Tom Jack didn't answer. He just started prowling around the store, as if he were searching for something. He looked behind counters and into the back room and finally he said to the feed salesman:

"If I could find me a wooden box, I'd show ya."

The salesman, fascinated by the notion of a girl taller than Tom Jack, joined eagerly in the search and at last they found a box that had contained a shipment of canned soup. Tom Jack placed it on the floor.

"Stand on it," he said, and the salesman did. Tom Jack stood off and sighted at him a moment and then said:

"Mister, you are now just about tall enough to kiss my sister's ass."

■   ■

George Lindsey, who plays the part of Goober on television's Andy Griffith show, says he was one of the few boys in his home town down in Alabama to go away to college. When he got home from school the first time his Paw demanded, "What did you learn?"

"Well," said George, "algebra."

"Say some," said Paw.

"Pi R square."

"Nope," said Paw. "Pie are round. *Cornbread* are square."

■ ■

In the same town, Mr. Lindsey reports, a fella was walkin'
down the street carryin' a sack with somethin' in it. Met another
fella. The other fella says:
 "Whatcha got in that sack?"
 "Chickens."
 "How many."
 "You guess how many an' I'll give you both of 'em."
 The fella studied a bit and then said:
 "Six?"

RECITATION NO. 4

(The late sportswriter Tom O'Reilly, as talented a storyteller as ever came down the pike, used to entertain us with this
recitation when Andy Griffith was still in grade school in Mount
Airy.)

Out in West Texas was a ranch about a hundred miles from a
town of any size. On this ranch lived two dozen cowhands and
not one of them had ever seen a football game. They had read
about football in old newspapers but they couldn't puzzle out the
difference between a halfback and an offside, or anything else
about the game. They were powerful curious.

One day they heard that a football game had been scheduled in
the town of Alpine a hundred miles from their ranch. Obviously
they all couldn't attend it, so they pooled up their money and
drew lots and one cowboy, named Ike, was chosen. He was to
get on his horse and ride the hundred miles to Alpine and see the
football game. Then he was to get on his horse and ride back
and tell the others all about it.

The cowboys were gathered at the gate when Ike came riding
back. They swarmed around him when he dismounted. What was
it like? How was it played? Was it exciting?

Ike called for quiet and then told his story, which went something like this:

"Fellers, this football is a caution. All I gotta do is tell you how the god-dang thing started off. They's a bunch of fellers in funny rig, out on this here field. They's a guy in a range-cook's outfit totin' a pig's bladder that's been blowed up and kivvered all around with cowhide. Well, these fellers all spreads out across the field and the range-cook puts the bladder on the ground and then one feller comes a-runnin' and kicks that bladder a helluva kick, clean up in the air.

"When it comes down they put it on the ground again. Then one great big feller walks up to that bladder and bends over like as if he's gonna pick it up. He hardly no more'n gits his hands on it when a little feller comes creepin' up behind him, all crouched over, sneaky-like, and this little feller gits closer and all of a sudden he bites this big feller right squar' in the ass and it turns into the God damndest fight you ever saw in yore life!"

BUSKIN' AT THE
CHECK-OUT COUNTER

The only reason I wish I were an actor is that actors are the best storytellers. The only reason I wish I were a Southerner is that Southerners are the second best. I actually *am* a Southerner, without being one. I come of a race that once inhabited the South and then moved away, evolving a pure and noble family strain out of corrupt beginnings.

It has been my good fortune to have wide associations with both actors and Confederates. Here is the way one particular Southern friend tells a story:

City Cousin went down to Georgia to visit Country Cousin. They fooled around some, went fishin', shot some pool, drank a good deal of cawn, got aholt of a bit of poon, and generally had a pleasant time.

Came the day when Country Cousin announced that it was time for a good old coon hunt. He had a coon hound named Old Blue and they lit into the woods. The procedure was like thisa here: every time Old Blue set to howlin' it meant he had a coon treed. Country Cousin would climb the tree and go out on the limb where the coon was and he'd shake the limb till the coon fell off.

The instant the coon hit the ground Old Blue was on it. First and *in*variable, that dog'd rape the coon. When he finished with that wild and crazy business, clawin' and floppin' around all over the clearin', he'd grab the coon by the neck and shake it to death.

They got one coon usin' this method, and then another, and then three more. Country Cousin decided they'd make a try for just one more and pretty soon Old Blue had him treed. Up the tree and out on the limb went Country Cousin. Further out and further out, and that limb kep' bendin' and kep' bendin' and Country Cousin was tryin' to be mighty careful, and then suddenly that limb begin to crack. The coon made a wild leap and landed on another branch, and City Cousin, seeing the way the limb was breaking, yelled up to Country Cousin:

"Country Cousin, what can I do to help you?"

And Country Cousin yelled down: "Nemmine me! Just git a good holt on Old Blue!"

■　　■

My representative in the half-world of jazz musicians is John Dengler. John has been my friend since his indiscreet days at Princeton, but lately he has given me so much trouble that I am thinking of striking him off my list. He wrote me from Fort Lauderdale that one of the most wonderful stories he ever heard ended with this line:

". . . while the butler sticks his dick in the mashed potatoes."

John said that strive as he might he could not remember the main body of the story that ended so provocatively. There was the faintest of tintinnabulations in my mind, but I could not come up with the first part of the story. I pondered it in the night, losing sleep over it, and finally phoned John in Florida. Had he found out what was going on elsewhere while the butler was sticking his dick in the mashed potatoes? He had not. He said that from time to time he gets desperate for the answer and calls people long distance all over the country about it. He said that the late editor Wilder Hobson strove mightily over the same riddle and was never able to find out what went before. So I intend to let it lay, right where it is. I don't want anybody telling me the answer. The proposition has reached the point where I think it is altogether sufficient, and satisfactory, that the butler sticks his dick in the mashed potatoes. His motive, if he had one, is of no consequence to me any longer.

■　■

A prominent political figure from England had been visiting in America and after an extensive tour of the New England States he declared that the town of East Horsham was his favorite community in that section of the country. He said that East Horsham seemed to him to be the "most typical New England town" of all those he had visited.

A star writer from one of our leading magazines was dispatched to East Horsham at once, along with a photographer. A prose poem in tribute to the community was in order. The Mayor took the visiting writer in hand and began a long tour of the Main Street, up one side and down the other, stopping often to discuss local history and regional lore and to meet the butcher, the baker, and the dealer in electrical appliances. This pedestrian coverage of the town went on for several hours and the New York writer noticed that there was one man, encountered from time to time, who was never introduced to him. The Mayor and other citizens appeared to shun this man like the Bubonic plague, though the man was neat-looking and conservatively dressed, and well-shaven and all. Still, he had a furtive and guilty look in his eye whenever he passed. Finally curiosity impelled the writer to speak about him.

"Why," he asked, "haven't you introduced me to that man who just walked by? And who is he?"

"I'm sorry you noticed him," said the Mayor. "I didn't want to *have* to speak of him. That's Burnaby Coatsworth, and I'd just as soon let it rest there, and say no more about him?"

"But why on earth do you scorn him like this?"

"Burnaby," said the Mayor, "dipped into his capital."

■　■

Jim Moran told me about the strength-testing machine in the Hollywood studio. It was devised and put together by an imaginative Texan and for several years it furnished great amusement for the people employed around this big radio studio at Hollywood and Vine.

It was a long box-like affair, standing about a foot off the floor, with a platform near the center for the feet. As a test of strength, a man would be instructed to stand on the platform, bend forward, seize a handle, and pull upward with all his might. Beside the handle, directly in front of the man's face, was a dial which registered his strength. Moran tried it himself. He had been rehearsing for a radio show and someone showed him the strength-testing machine.

"I always fancied myself as being strong," he said, "and so I got on it and bent over and took a good grip on that handle and then gave it all I had. Great God! The things that happened! A plank came up from behind and hit me a helluva belt right in the ass. At the same instant I got an electrical shock from the handle that almost took my hands off at the wrists. Simultaneously a .45 revolver went off inside the box and a stream of icy water shot up from that dial and hit me square in the face. It all happened at once. They had to take me home and put me to bed. Most unnerving thing that ever happened to me. They kept this machine around for wise guys, especially some of the Hollywood hams who come in and talk big and make life miserable for everyone else. Those are the very kind of people who'll bite on a thing like that—a chance to show off their muscles. I saw several of them get it later on. It really shatters people. They remain sheeplike, and sort of numb, for a week or more. They don't talk biggety for quite a while."

■ ■

A world-famous motion picture actress, living in one of those Beverly Hills palaces and newly married to a handsome gent who was a novelist, came home from her studio one afternoon feeling blithe and gay.

Bounding into the house she went up the wide stairway two steps at a time and entered the master bedroom where she flung her purse and her script on a table and then noted that the shower was running in the bath. She stepped into the bathroom, slid the glass door open a foot, reached in through the vapor and splashing water, groped about until she found what she was seeking, gave it a couple of yanks and cried out, "Ding dong bell!"

Then she went tripping out through the bedroom into the upper hallway and on the stairway . . . ran into her husband.

■   ■

A Park Avenue lady, wife of a well-heeled corporation lawyer (was there ever a *poorly* heeled one?), stepped into a Manhattan pet shop to get a set of military brushes for her spaniel. While waiting her turn, she noticed a very peculiar bird. Its blue body was no bigger than that of a pigeon but it had a huge head and long powerful-looking jaws like a pelican.

The lady asked the shopkeeper what kind of a bird it was and he said it was a crunch bird. She remarked on its surpassing ugliness and then asked why it had the name of crunch bird.

"I'll show you," said the shopkeeper. He opened the gate of the cage and spoke. "Crunch bird," he called out, "the table."

The bird stepped out of the cage, spread his ugly little wings, flapped swiftly across the room to a rather heavy table, opened his jaws wide, fastened them onto the table, and crrrrrrr-unch! He bit a wedge of wood out of the table as if it had been made of Camembert cheese. The bird dropped the chunk of wood on the floor and immediately returned to his cage.

The lady, after a few moments of thought, said she wanted to buy that bird. The proprietor said it was not for sale. It was the only crunch bird in captivity, and he was keeping it for his own pleasure. The lady insisted, and began mentioning attractive sums of money, and upping the bid as the man continued in his determination not to sell.

When at last she arrived at ten thousand dollars the shopkeeper gave her a long searching look.

"Tell you what I'll do," he said. "I'll let you take it, provided you tell me honestly why you would pay that much dough for such an ugly, mean, destructive creature."

"Sure, I'll tell you," she said. "I have a husband who is the Number One Wise Guy of the earth. He knows all the answers. He is the greatest living authority on everything. On top of that, he's the meanest son of a bitch that ever put on socks. If I had this bird I could fix his wagon."

"How?" the shopkeeper wanted to know.

"I'd take the bird home and put the cage in the living room and when I heard my husband coming I'd open the cage door. So he'd come in, the mean bastard, growling and grouching as usual. He'd take off his coat and throw it on the floor and rip off his tie and fling it across the room and he'd mutter all kinds of nasty curses and then he'd see the cage. He'd say, 'What in Christ's name is that?' And I'd say, 'That's a crunch bird.' And Mister Wise Guy would snort in derision, and say in a loud voice: '*Crunch bird my ass!*'"

■   ■

Politicians would appear to be the same the wide world over. In rural Connecticut there was a farmer named Boyd who decided to run for county office. A leader of his political party in the county seat thought he'd make a few inquiries and one day spotted another farmer, a neighbor of Boyd, buying some nails at the hardware botique. He approached this old man and asked him what he thought of Boyd as a candidate for public office. The farmer ran his hand through his beard and looked wise and said nothing.

"Would you say he's an honest man," the questioner persisted, "or would you rate him as a liar?"

The old farmer considered for a few moments and then answered slowly: "I wouldn't go so fur as to call him a liar, but I've heered tell that when he wants his pigs to come in for their feedin', he has to git somebody else to call 'em."

■   ■

There was a Vermont farmer whose home place was close to the New Hampshire border. A survey was undertaken for a new highway, and it brought the disclosure that the farm actually had always been on the New Hampshire side of the line. Advised of this, the farmer said:

"Well, thank the good God Almighty. I couldn't have stood another one of them Vermont winters."

■　■
　　　My father never found anything amusing about anything I ever said or anything I ever wrote (I heard that, you snotty bastards!) except for one story I told him. It was about a man who inherited a couple of million dollars while he was attending Harvard. He quit college and began traveling. He traveled all over the world and continued his travels up to the age of seventy, at which point a reporter called upon him to interview him. The reporter finally asked him which city, of all the cities he had visited, he liked the best. He didn't hesitate. He said Venice. The reporter asked him why. "It's the only city I was ever in," he said, "where a man can sit in a saloon and fish out the window."

That story puts me in mind of an English character named Walking Stewart, whose career was called to my attention when I was doing research in London. Stewart went out to Inja as a clark, but wearied of his work, threw over his job, and walked from Calcutta to France. His idea was simply to get home but now he discovered that he liked to walk, so he walked all over the rest of Europe and then walked all over the United States. After he had covered the greater part of the globe on foot he, too, was interviewed, it being thought that he would have some interesting observations to make on the state of civilization. The reporters pressed him hard, but he said he hadn't observed much of anything and had no thoughts worth recounting. He hadn't kept notes or a diary. The reporters hammered at him, insisting that he must have arrived at some conclusions about the state of the world, and finally Walking Stewart spoke this judgment:

"I think the time will come when ladies of breeding will quit bearing children, and only the poor people will have families."

■　■
　　　I had lunch one day with some people at a restaurant on Kalakauau Avenue in Waikiki. Among those present was a strikingly attractive woman, a woman with whom I had become casually acquainted, a woman who had class, and charm, and great poise, and who was drinking vodka. She told us she was divorced, and she spoke well of her former husband.

"We have continued to be good friends," she said. "He is a genuinely warm person, a real wonderful guy—it's just that our interests are not the same. It's so much better when there is none of that awful bitterness."

She had another vodka.

"Of course," she said, "we had our little quarrels, like everyone else. But at the same time we had respect for each other. A great guy—a real great guy!"

She had another vodka. She talked some more, glowingly, of the great guy, and then she had another vodka. After a while she had still another and her tongue was getting a trifle thick. She spread her elbows on the table and ordered more vodka and just before we departed she fastened a hard, glaring, glassy eye on me and said:

"I tell you *this*, my fine-feathered friend. Let that dirty son of a bidge miss just *one* alimony payment and by God I break it off in him, the no-good cheap bassard! I'll fraggsure the son of a bitch's stoopid goddamn skull off!"

One encounters many interesting personalities in Waikiki.

■   ■

In Cro-Magnon times, when men had very long heads with low orbits, I interviewed Gary Cooper in the New York headquarters of Samuel Goldwyn's film company. I don't remember a single thing that was said during that interview, because it culminated in an incident that somewhat overshadowed it.

When the session was over I stopped at the men's room on my way to the elevator. Gary Cooper was just coming out. In a moment I found myself inside, standing alongside an office boy. He turned his head to me, grinned broadly, and said:

"Right on top of Gary Cooper's!"

■   ■

Louis Untermeyer tells of the traveler driving through the Kentucky hills and coming upon a farmer holding a large pig in his arms. The wayfarer stopped to observe the scene more carefully and found that the farmer was holding the pig so the animal could eat the apples right off the tree.

"Won't it take you a long time to fatten your hog that way?" suggested the traveler.

"Spose so," agreed the farmer, "but what's time to a dern hawg?"

■　　■

The only reason I keep on working is that I have an eagerness to get my hands on some more of that mazuma. Mazuma is a slang word used by the hippies and the teeny-boppers and the jet-setters as meaning kale, cabbage, long green. And the reason I want some more mazuma is that I enjoy spending it on travel. As much roving around as I do, I must confess that the business of taking trips can be fraught with foul-ups, and that you have to expect unpleasant happenings along the way. I've written whole books about the alarums that have been my lot in faraway places, and near.

Hugh Downs had a small crisis once when he and his wife Ruth were attending a conference of television executives in Washington. When the time came for the flight back to New York, the weather had turned bad and it was necessary to take a train. From his room Hugh phoned the travel desk and they said they could get him and Mrs. Downs on the five o'clock train, which would be leaving in an hour. Ruth was in the bathroom so Hugh hurriedly packed the bags, throwing his things and her things in helter-skelter, and then he called the bell captain and asked if the bags could be rushed right over to the depot and put on the train. A boy came immediately and got them.

A couple of minutes later Mrs. Downs stepped out of the bathroom, wrapped in a towel, and said: "Dear, would you please hand me my green dress?"

■　　■

Wait! Don't say it! I'll kill anybody who says it! I am still concerned with the preceding Hugh Downs story. It is the precise kind of story that brings forth the punchline-tromp.

Among all the insensible and witless lardheads in the world, this fellow (or girl) is about the worst. In almost any crowd where the storytelling is going along good, a punchline-tromper is likely to pop in view. He is the fellow who, at the end of the Hugh Downs story, where Mrs. Downs asks for her green dress, breaks in with:

"So what happened?"

My considered advice is that whenever you encounter a punchline-tromper, you should strangle him. Everyone present should take part in the ceremony; make certain he stays strangled. Then go to court and tell the judge: "The bastard said, 'So what happened?' at the punchline of a story." The case will be dismissed instanter.

■   ■

    A portion of this story was told to me once in South Carolina. The second part I heard at various times in Mexico City, in Los Angeles, and standing on the shore of Walden Pond in Massachusetts. In Waikiki, however, the locale was Hawaiian and the parts had been deftly joined in a single incident.

There was this Hawaiian girl from the island of Maui who came to Honolulu seeking a job as a stenographer. She was given a form to fill out. She came to the line: "Present position." She studied it a moment and wrote in: "Sitting down." And where it said "Sex" she wrote, in a laudable burst of integrity: "Once, in Kipahulu."

■   ■

    There is a story about Addison Mizner, brother of the more celebrated Wilson Mizner, with a setting in San Francisco's Golden Gate Park. Addison, as a young man, was rejected by a girl with whom he was madly in love. He decided to do away with himself. He acquired a pistol and got on a streetcar and rode out to the park. He walked about for a while until he found a secluded spot which he decided was esthetically correct for self-destruction. He sat down and got out his gun and composed himself for some final thoughts. The first final thought to hit him was that he had quite a large hole torn in his underpants. He loosened his belt and reached in and verified the existence of the rip. My God, he told himself, he couldn't be found dead in *that* condition. He'd have to go home and change his drawers and then come back and do his suicide. So he got back on the streetcar and on the way to his home it occurred to him that the damn girl wasn't worth all the bother, and he went on to become a colorful important figure in architecture and in the social life of boomtime Palm Beach.

We've all heard of this type of conceit, which is exemplified by the old lady who always dresses for the coroner. She fears that she may drop dead with a hole in her stocking or soiled underwear. This fear becomes almost an obsession with her and she even readies herself for the coroner when she goes to bed at night.

I wonder if it doesn't affect us all. Not long ago I was writing a novel in which the central character was a cat. There were a lot of people in the story but the cat, he was the . . . well, the catalyst of the drama. He was not a talking animal—just a big ornery cat with a jog in his tail. His tail defect served him as an instrument for expressing emotion. When the jog in his tail began to jerk, that cat was overwrought about something.

As I worked along on this story I found myself now and then getting so involved with the people that I was neglecting the cat. It was necessary that, from time to time, I bring the cat back into the story, if only to remind the reader that he was still around. And the easiest way for me to call attention to his presence was to have him move that tail to indicate that he was taking some kind of an interest in things.

I took a large sheet of cardboard and a marking pencil and printed in big letters:

JERK THAT TAIL!

I hung this sign on the wall directly opposite my desk so I would see it each time I looked up. It would remind me to get that cat back into the story.

I looked at it, I think, maybe twice. Then it dawned on me.

What if I keeled over dead of a heart attack right at my typewriter? What would they think if . . . ?

And it took me back to another incident. I once wrote a book with the title, *The Age of the Tail*. Around the publishing business a book is usually called by one word out of its title. That one was always referred to as "Tail." It had been published several months and a Broadway producer was toying with the idea of rendering it into a musical comedy.

One day I took the train in to Manhattan to take care of another matter. I had made a note on a slip of paper as a reminder that I wanted to find out what that producer was doing. Sitting on the train I pulled the note out of my pocket and read it. It said: "Check Tail Situation."

I sat and looked at it a minute or two, and then tore it into tiny pieces and threw the pieces away. It came to me in a flash, my death in that railroad car, and the Medical Examiner arriving, and the cops, and they would go through my clothes and find that note, and look at it a bit, and then someone would say: "The poor son of a bitch! On his way into town to get laid!"

■   ■

There is a great surfeit of jokes about women drivers. Among the later ones, I like best the story of the husband who arrived at the main highway, with his wife at his side, and prepared to make a left turn onto the pavement.

"Look your way," he ordered. "Any cars coming?"

"No."

He started to make his turn when she added:

"Only a truck."

■   ■

I think it was my old friend Beverly Smith of the *Saturday Evening Post* who once undertook a nationwide tour for the purpose of sampling the grub in the nation's most famous restaurants.

Both Beverly and his wife were eatin' people and for them it was an enjoyable assignment. They arrived in Charleston, South

Carolina, and after freshening up at their hotel hurried out for dinner at one of the town's leading taverns.

A grizzled Negro waiter (there has never in history been an ungrizzled one) stood by to take their order. In his slow-talkin' way he told them to take their time, and so they studied the menu, and finally Mrs. Smith spoke.

"What," she asked, "is the soup du jour?"

"Cow pea soup, ma'am."

She showed only slight distress as she looked across at Beverly.

"Well," she said with an air of resignation, "I promised that I'd be willing to try *anything*, so bring it on."

■   ■

On another occasion I think I mentioned that certain objects are funny in themselves—a mule, for example. Almost any story with a gorilla in it is comical. But what the hell is so funny about green beans?

On reflection, I now seem to recall that green beans are funny *only* when mentioned in connection with a traveling salesman stopping overnight at a farmhouse where there is a pretty daughter or sometimes a lustful young wife.

I heard my first such story in the time when the Düsenberg was the *in* car. A salesman stopped at a farmhouse and for supper there was a great bowl of green beans. They were tasty, and the visitor ate helping after helping, and they got to calling him Mr. Green Beans in a kidding way. At last all went to bed, and in the night the farmer's pretty young daughter called out: "Paw! Oh Paw! Green beans lies heavy on my stomach tonight!" And Paw hollered back, "Well, git up and git yourself a dose of bakin' powder."

In the present era, the drama has no pretty daughter in the cast, but an eager young wife. The salesman and the farmer and the pretty young wife enjoy a bait of green beans for supper, and the salesman speaks frequently of how good they are, complimenting the wife on them and pleasing her no end. All three sleep that night in the same room. In the night the wife nudges her husband awake and tells him some animal is prowling around the henhouse, so the farmer gets up and slips on his pants and shoes and goes outdoors. The moment he has gone his wife calls across the room: "Now's your chance!" And the salesman jumps out of bed and hurries to the kitchen to get himself some more of those good green beans.

It may come as a sort of anticlimax to tell one without green beans in it, but the most recent variation to reach my ear involves *two* traveling salesmen, and no farmer at all. These two salesmen arrived at the lonely but handsome farmhouse and were welcomed by an attractive young widow, who fixed supper for them and told them that her husband died a year ago, and that she has been living alone in the big house. She gave them separate bedrooms upstairs and in the morning served them a fine breakfast and they went on their way. Several months later the two men were recalling the incident and one said:

"Tell me something. Did you get up in the night and sneak downstairs to her bedroom?"

"Yeah."

"And did you tell her you were me? Give her *my* name?"

"Yeah. Gee, I'm sorry! I didn't think . . ."

"Don't feel sorry about it. I just got a letter from her lawyer. She died last week and left me the farm."

John F. Kennedy enjoyed ragging his associates, especially when he was in the presidential chair. It is told on somewhat shabby authority that he was discussing the eminent Arthur J. Goldberg, then a justice of the Supreme Court and later United States Ambassador to the United Nations. President Kennedy said that Justice Goldberg had been inveigled into going with a group of friends on a mountain-climbing expedition in the Alps.

The party was well up in the mountains when someone noticed that Arthur Goldberg was missing. A search was undertaken, but he couldn't be found, and someone was sent down to fetch professional help. Up from the village came a team of Red Cross workers and they joined in the search. One member of this group was scrambling around on the side of an Alp when he thought he detected a movement up above.

He yelled: "Goldberg! Goldberg! It's the Red Cross!"

And the response came down the mountainside: "I gave at the office!"

■ ■

A large and glittering convertible pulled up at a bus stop where a cute young girl, a stenographer with a build, was waiting for her bus. At the wheel of the car was a male person of the type sometimes categorized as weisenheimer.

"Hi!" he said to the girl, flashing his teeth and exuding confidence. "I'm driving west."

"Oh, how nice," said the girl. "Bring me back an orange."

■ ■

I can remember once when I was in the home of the late Ben Bernie and Mrs. Bernie was telling me that The Old Maestro was so devout a fan of racehorses that he demanded that their wedding be held in Seabiscuit's stable, and that their wedding picture be taken with the horse standing between them.

That sounds a bit of all right with me, but I do think that a devotion to sports can be carried too far. John Bainbridge once wrote about how sporting events make up Toots Shor's frame of reference. Shor was once talking about how he got his restaurant started. "I signed the lease," he said, "on September 15th, 1939— the day Galento beat Nova, in Philadelphia." He enjoys recalling his first wedding anniversary. "One of the biggest upsets in football happened that day," says Shor. "Notre Dame beat Ohio State. What a game! Notre Dame scored two touchdowns in the last minute and a half of play." Of course he has a vivid memory of the night his first child was born: "It was right after Beau Jack beat Fritzie Zivic the second time, at the Garden—a good fight."

■ ■

Speaking of athletics, there was this man who was watching a ball game in which one son was playing on one team, and another son on the other. Someone asked him which team he was rooting for. He said that he felt a good deal like the Tennessee farmer who was lolling on the front porch of his mountain cabin when his eye fell on a brisk bit of action out in the road—his wife was engaged in a fierce hand-to-hand struggle with a large bear. Said the hillbilly:

"Ah do bleeve this here's the fust fight Ah ever seen whirr Ah don't give a damn which un wins."

■   ■

Henry Mencken once proposed a law under which, immediately after each Presidential election, the loser be taken out immediately and hanged. This was Mr. Mencken's way of saying that the losing candidate usually starts buzzing around after his defeat and making an eternal nuisance out of himself.

There are many who believe that Herbert Hoover lacked a sense of humor. I incline toward that opinion, though a story was told about him during his first week in office that at least had a suggestion of wit. Mr. Hoover told an old friend that he felt there ought to be a law under which the President would be allowed to hang two men every year without giving any reason or explanation.

"Would two be enough?" asked the friend, a realist.

"Perhaps not," said Mr. Hoover, "but I could get word to twenty or thirty that they were being considered for the honor."

RECITATION NO. 5

Beauty comes to me in strange places, and with it inspiration. I was in St. Petersburg, Florida, on my way down the Gulf Coast, when I picked up a local paper and came upon a column written by Sydney J. Harris. Mr. Harris writes out of Chicago and is one of our more literate and entertaining newspaper guys. I don't think he knew how well he entertained me on this particular day in St. Petersburg. On second thought, maybe he *did* know. His column was concerned with book titles, and was in the form of an open letter.

As I read it, for some strange reason the aforementioned beauty and inspiration struck me, and where Mr. Harris had put in blanks, I put in a four-letter word, or variations of that word. I am not going to reprint his whole column, but I'll give you enough of it to entertain *you*. Maybe. Here goes:

> DEAR Book Publishers—If you have any forthcoming books in your spring list which fall into the following categories, please do not send me advance copies:
> Any book with the title, "So You're Going to ——."
> Any book with the title, "I Was a ——."
> Any book with the title, "Ten Ways to ——."
> Any book with the title, "The —— Story."
> Any book with the title, "You Can ——."
> Any book with the title, "A Treasury of ——."
> Any book with the title, "The Immortal ——."
> Any book with the title, "—— at the Crossroads."
> Any book with the title, "The Fabulous ——."
> Any book with the title, "Inside ——."
> Any book with the title, "The Unknown ——."
> Any book with the title, "The Man Who ——."
> Any book with the title, "Twenty Years a ——."
> Any book with the title, "Secrets of ——."
> Any book with the title, "——, City of ——."
> Any book with the title, "—— For All Occasions."
> Any book with the title, "Whither ——?"

I passed this little word-game along to a lady who works at *Time* and who is an old friend, and she and some of her associates took it from there, and even got out the endless lists of cookbooks on the market today, and began substituting what we call "Our Word" for the word "cooking." I enjoyed particularly their book titled, "—— With Sour Cream."

ANECDOTES THAT USUALLY
GO GOOD IN
AN ABANDONED MINE SHAFT

There exists among us a type of man who appears to get a mild pleasure out of listening to stories, but who is dead serious about everything in life and usually smokes a pipe. When someone has finished telling him a real good story he'll chuckle, just to prove that he *got* it, and that he sees all the fun in it, and then he's likely to take the pipe out of his mouth and make a few Socratic grimaces with his mouth and jaws and glance at the ceiling and then say: "I often wonder just where all these stories originate. Who creates them? No one ever seems to know."

He's right about one thing—no one ever seems to know. That is, no one but a stockbroker friend of John Dengler, who says with an authoritative air: "All jokes are written, composed, or narrated in the town of Valdosta, Georgia. Every damn one of them, without exception."

Dengler asked this stockbroker to give him an example of a joke that originated in Valdosta, Georgia. Without hesitation the man said: "What has four thousand legs, two cherries, and flies? You don't know? Two thousand airline stewardesses."

So, let us be satisfied with life as it is, and try not to complicate our existence with minor worries. There are all manner of evil individuals to be encountered in the world of storytelling. Not forgetting our old friend the punchline-tromper, the son of a bitch who at the conclusion of that stockbroker's riddle, would have asked: "Which airline?"

■ ■

I am unable to tell if the following item had its origin in Valdosta, Georgia. I do know that a friend of mine, traveling in the West, sent it to me from Arizona. He went into a Mexican restaurant in Tombstone, and this Mexican restaurant was called The Oriental, and the management put the following composition on each table, as if it were a doily:

A big business man was sitting at a bar drinking beer when a girl came in and sat on a stool next to him. He looked her over and started conversation. He soon propositioned her and offered her $1,000 to spend the week-end with him at his home. Thinking how nice the $1,000 would be, she accepted. After the week-end was over and they started home, she asked him for the money and he said he'd mail a check for the amount.

The check arrived but it was only for $500. So she decided to call on him at his office. It was full of people and not wanting to embarrass him she said: "In regard to that house you rented—I only received half the rent." The man, catching on, said: "Oh yes, the house; well, in the first place, you didn't tell me it had been used. In the second place, it was too big, and in the third place, there was no heat." She then replied, saying: "In the first place you didn't ask if it had been used. In the second place it wasn't too big, you just didn't have enough furniture to fill it; and in the third place there was plenty of heat—you just didn't know how to turn it on." She got the $500.

■ ■

After a year of service in Vietnam, young Lafe Weehunt came home to the Ozarks, ready to take up his work again on the family's hillside farm. Lafe didn't come home empty-handed; he had a little loot with him, including a chemical toilet. The first time he saw one in Vietnam he knew it was the very thing that was needed back home, and so he managed to tote one back with him, along with some other odds and ends.

Soon after his arrival home he got the toilet installed in the house and then, wondering what to do with the old privy, he remembered that he had half a dozen sticks of dynamite in his footlocker, along with the mechanism for setting them off. He got the dynamite and rigged it beneath the outhouse and strung some wires down the hillside and he was hooking up the circuit when Grandpap came out of the kitchen door and hit a beeline for the privy. Unhappily, his grandson didn't see him.

Pretty soon Lafe was all set, and rammed down the plunger, and BUH-LOOOOOEY! Splinters filled the sky, flying in all directions, and as the smoke cleared Lafe saw that Grandpap had been dynamited along with everything else, and was lying on the ground forty feet from the scene of the blast.

Lafe rushed to the old man's side just in time to see him get to his knees and then slowly stand up.

"You hurt, Grandpap?" he cried.

"Nawp," said Grandpap, slowly. "Don't think so. But boy, one thing ah'll tell you, Ah'm shore glad Ah didn't try to slide that one out in the kitchen!"

■　■

Most of you, I imagine, can remember when Robert Briscoe was the Jewish Lord Mayor of Dublin, and how he came over to New York and led the St. Patrick's Day parade down Fifth Avenue. *That* Paddy's Day procession had an audience!

On the sidelines were two elderly Jewish ladies who had come down from the Bronx to witness this great spectacle. When Lord Mayor Briscoe hove into view, they were beside themselves with pride.

"Looka!" said one lady. "Lord Mayor fomm a heff million Irishmens!"

Her friend sighed with satisfaction and murmured: "Could only heppening in America!"

■　■

Toward the end of his life George S. Kaufman said that he had enjoyed things because he had followed the only piece of advice his father had ever given him: "Son, try everything in life except incest and folk-dancing."

A Kaufman anecdote with a bite to it concerned the bill a man got from his lawyer which said: "For crossing street to speak to you and discovering it was not you—$12."

■　■

A goodly crowd of the Beautiful People was present one afternoon in the cocktail lounge of a fashionable New York hotel. A solemn waiter crossing the floor suddenly stumbled and fell forward. A tall drink on his tray, loaded with ice cubes, was dumped right down the back of a lady at one of the tables— inside her gown.

She gave forth a mannerly screech, then began writhing in her chair like a wounded python, gasping and giggling and letting out whinnies and yelps; then she leaped to her feet, accidentally knocking her gentleman companion to the floor, and she was doing a composite of several of the new jerk-dances when he managed to get up and lead her from the room.

Another gentleman with a lady at a nearby table now called the waiter. He ordered: "Bring us two of whatever it was they had."

■　■

Anybody here happen to know Hedda Hopper's real name? Elda Furry. She always said she'd have stayed with it and worn it with pride, if it hadn't happened that she married De Wolf Hopper back in 1913. She was his fifth wife. "To know him," she said, "was to marry him." His previous wives had been named Ella, Ida, Edna and Nella—and here was Elda coming along to confound the confusion. "I changed it to Hedda," she said, "because I was afraid he wouldn't know who I was."

■　■

Some of you may recall that back yonder I mentioned the skill which the average actor has in telling stories. I've also spoken of the popular interdiction against anyone ever discussing religion, politics or sex. Yet I find that my ears always prick up when an actor or an actress begins talking religion. Show biz people seem to embrace such enchanting religious views, and they are somehow able to enunciate them so eloquently.

I suppose almost everyone has heard of Jane Russell's response to the question, "Just how do you visualize God?" She said: "When you get to know Him, He's just a livin' doll!"

I once heard Mel Allen say on the air: "On this beautiful Memorial Day, let us all give thanks to the Lord that we're able to look at this double-header."

And I remember the time when Arthur Godfrey was being interviewed by Marie Torre, and he got to talking soft and purty about life and birds and flowers and God and other things that he knows about, and then he said: "Everlasting life? You're darn tootin' there is!"

I once read a newspaper review of a western movie starring Steve McQueen, who played the role of a vengeful killer. At one point in the story a priest showed him a Bible and then a crucifix. The killer stared at the crucifix a long while and then said: "That looks worse'n hangin'."

Some day when I can get around to it, I am going to do a *special*, like in TV, on Theology as Made Clear by Georgie Jessel. You'll bust a gut.

■   ■

The Duke of Windsor's life story has lately been put on film, with special emphasis on his romance with Wallace Simpson. There are, apparently, a few things missing from the picture, although I'm told that in the commentary the Duke said he always tried to follow the advice: "Never miss an opportunity to sit down and never miss an opportunity to relieve yourself."

This somehow fits (or doesn't fit) the story I've heard about how the Duke, whenever he was dining at fashionable Le Pavillon in New York, went sporadically to the can, and each time he did, the proprietor of the establishment, Henri Soule, always stood guard at the swinging door. Nobody was allowed to see the Duke go.

There are two small anecdotes I can remember about him. When he was the Prince of Wales he visited the United States, amid great pomp and ceremony, and during his stay in Philadelphia someone asked him if he had yet run into any Biddles. "No," he replied, "I believe not. What *is* a biddle?"

In later years he was touring through the Pratt & Whitney plant in Connecticut and George Dixon, writing an account of it, said that at one point during the tour the Duke slipped on an oily spot and almost fell on his whitney. In those times that was about as insanely daring as a newspaper writer could get.

■   ■

As I was talking about the Duke of Windsor's reluctance to have witnesses around whenever he was facing up to the vitreous china, there was a faint clang. The bell that it rang took me back to the books, and the splendid regime of Louis XIV.

Like Windsor, this Louis had his moments of modesty. It had been the custom in many royal courts of Europe to permit privileged individuals to stand in the presence of the King while he was performing his morning duties. It was among the most cherished privileges of the court to watch His Highness strain and groan and grunt. You don't believe it? Go check the historical records of etiquette and protocol among the Kings of France and Spain as well as the rulers of Germany.

In some courts the thing got out of hand and so many people crowded into the room that there was danger of suffocation. Louis XIV decided that the witnesses should be restricted in number, and he specified under hand and seal that they should include princesses and princes of the blood, the Ministers, Madame de Maintenon (natch!), certain lawgivers and church dignitaries and military leaders, and the *porte-chaise d'affaires,* who had the high honor of carrying the thronelike can in and out of the royal chambers.

Much importance was attached to this portable piece of furniture, called the *chaise percée* (chair with an opening in the wood). According to Paul Tabori, Catherine de Medici had one lined in blue and one in red velvet, and after her husband died she had a third tatted up, nicely upholstered in black.

Also, according to Mr. Tabori, some royal personages would

never dream of performing their rites anywhere but upon the one noble john. Whenever Ferdinand IV, King of Naples, went to the theater a special detachment of the royal guards carried his toilet from the palace to the royal box and back and Mr. Tabori says that whenever the thing passed in the streets, soldiers saluted it smartly, and officers stood at rigid attention, with swords drawn.

We don't do things up that good anymore.

■   ■

Whenever Goodman Ace talks about his old friend Al Boasberg, he speaks with a certain reverence. Boasberg was a comedy writer and a giant among wits. Once he and Ace went to the movies and in the middle of the picture Boasberg suddenly stood up and asked in a loud voice: "Is there a Christian Scientist in the house?" A woman on the other side of the theater arose and called back: "I'm a Christian Scientist." And Boasberg said: "Would you mind changing seats with me? I'm sitting in a draft."

■   ■

My old Broadway crony Ben Serkowich told me once that he had been worrying about the amount of drinking he had been doing. He had to go to a cocktail party, put on by his movie studio, and so he decided to try a new technique. "If I kept saying to myself," he recalled, "that I was not going to let the stuff affect me, and say it over and over and over, and keep my mind on it all the time, then I would not get stiff. So I did it, and damned if it didn't seem to work beautifully, and I just kept belting away, and suddenly I plunged forward to the floor . . . and when I woke up the next morning . . . it was four days later."

■   ■

In the wooded hills of North Westchester we lead a slightly different kind of life than people of many other regions. We pride ourselves on our moral fibre. We are people in the arts and the professions and most of us commute five days a week to New York City. In the summertime each weekend sees a great migration of our friends and fellow workers, fleeing from the heat and dirt of New York City. Many of them don't appreciate the joys of life in exurbia and some are perplexed by it. Oliver Herford, whose wit once enlivened the Manhattan literary world, was having breakfast in the country home of a friend when he noticed a comb of honey on the table. "Ah," he said, "I see you keep a bee." And S. N. Behrman, the playwright, once complained about weekends in the country, saying he despised them "because the air always seems to be full of uncooked birds."

One of the more inspirational tales reflecting our moral tone begins with a stock salesman boarding a commuter train at Pleasantville after spending the weekend at the home of friends. Another man, just ahead of him, takes the window seat and the Wall Street man sits down beside him. The train window is open, and the other passenger is talking to a man on the station platform. From the conversation it is easy to determine that the one has been the weekend guest of the other. A moment or two before the train pulls out the man on the train says loudly to his friend:

"It was real great, Fred, real great. And I want you to know that your wife is just as fine a lay as I ever had in my life."

The train moved, and our stock salesman didn't hear what was said from the station platform. He was, however, greatly astonished at what he had heard and as the train moved southward he continued thinking about it. Maybe he actually hadn't heard it. He decided to find out.

"Pardon me," he said to his seatmate. "I don't want to be rude but I'm just dying of curiosity about something I think I heard you say back there, to your friend on the station platform. Did you tell him that his wife was a fine lay?"

"Yes," said the other man. "I told him she was. She really isn't. It's just that he's *such* a sweet guy!"

■   ■

Buddy Hackett says that his wife told him one day that they ought to join a Temple.

"Why?" demanded Buddy.

"So our children will know they're Jewish."

"They know they're Jewish," said Buddy. "They got heartburn all the time."

Buddy speaks often and feelingly about food. Once when Jack Paar was uttering a commercial for Adolph's Meat Tenderizer, Buddy broke in with: "I tried it, but I had to give it up. I eat slow, and it was tenderizing my lips."

■ ■

One evening a while back I was sitting in a popular seafood restaurant on the outskirts of Corpus Christi, Texas, a town with nice outskirts, and across the table from me was a ruddy Texan, a man with an honest face and a forthright manner. He said he was well aware of the fact that I was always on the prowl for stories of one kind or another, and that he had a pretty fair one.

"It is a true story," he said, "and I know it's true because it happened in Denton which is my home town and I was back there to visit some kinfolks of mine recently, and I got in on the tail-end of it." I now proceed with this story as this Denton gentleman told it with high-heeled boots on.

In Denton there was a man named McCaleb who ran a concrete products company, dealing largely in what Texans call see-ment. One of those firms that has see-ment mixers mounted on trucks and doing the mixing as they proceed along the highways to various construction jobs. This man McCaleb's see-ment business was flourishing and he lived in a fine mansion and rode around in an air-conditioned Cadillac.

Came a time when McCaleb met a lovely young married creature and went on the make for her and made her and liked it and decided he wanted a lot more. She had a husband who worked as a machinist, but was momentarily unemployed, so this McCaleb came up with a great idea. He would hire the husband to drive one of his see-ment trucks, and he would arrange to have the husband jockey a see-ment truck to some job on the far side of town on those afternoons when McCaleb wanted to call on the wife. That way he would always feel pretty sure that the assignations wouldn't be discovered.

Things went along beautifully, and without a hitch, and then came an afternoon, one of McCaleb's poon days, when the see-ment-headed cuckold left the plant with his mixer loaded, headed for the far side of town. It popped into his mind that he needed to pick up some papers involving the mortgage on his home, and so he drove his see-ment truck to the house. There at the curb stood the boss's Cadillac.

He got down from his truck and crept around back and peeked in a bedroom window and there they were. They weren't playing parcheesi. The husband went back to his truck and stood in thought, uncertain about what he ought to do, and then his eye fell on the Cadillac. Keeping as quiet as possible, he backed his truck around, wheeled down one window of the Cadillac just enough to get the big hose in, and then he filled the big car almost to the brim with see-ment. Following which he drove back to the plant.

That's the story. No, the man from Denton had a postscript. The story of the Cadillac full of see-ment was all over Denton. McCaleb evidently spirited the shameful thing away in the middle of the night, for it was nowhere in evidence. Everyone was asking, "So what *happened* to the Cadillac full of see-ment?" A few days passed and then a smart Chevrolet dealer put up a tent on his used-car lot. On the tent he placed a sign: SEE THE CAR WITH THE CEMENT IN IT! And people came flocking to the tent, so they could tell their grandchildren later on how they had seen the actual car. Inside the tent was the latest model Impala —which hadn't been moving too well for the local dealer—and standing in the back seat, two bags of Portland see-ment. A fine bit of promotion.

Now. I really enjoyed hearing that story and made notes about it and even began thinking of building a short story around it, for some magazine. After I got home a magazine editor gently informed me that the Cadillac full of see-ment was the most common of all those stories which achieve an enormous circula-tion and which are invariably told by people who claim the incident happened to them, personally, or to a friend of their cousin's, or to a neighbor. Later on I learned that Jack Paar had told the story on his television show, only to find out that every person over seven years old in the entire country already knew it; and Paar himself discovered that a Canadian newspaperman had tried to trace it down to its origin, without success, and Bob Sylvester in New York did the same.

■   ■

As I said, this type of tale appears with such frequency that there are enough of them to make a book. Seems to me that the late Alexander Woollcott did an essay about them. They are almost always exceptionally good stories, but the one strange characteristic about them is the fact that the teller invariably says they happened to him, or to a friend, or to a relative, and he or she is willing to swear a mighty oath that they are true. One that I've always enjoyed, which made the wires of the Associated Press and which Paar quoted in one of his books, went this way (in the AP version):

A motorist from Cranston, R. I., sheepishly swears this story is true . . . He was driving on the Merritt Parkway when his battery died. He flagged down a woman driver, and she agreed to give him a push to start his car. Because his car had an automatic transmission, he explained to her that she would have to get up to thirty or thirty-five miles an hour to get him started.

The lady nodded wisely. The stalled driver climbed into his car and waited for her to line up behind him. He waited and waited. Then he turned around to see where she was. She was there all right—bearing down on him at thirty-five miles an hour.

Damage to his car: three hundred dollars.

My neighbors of the *Reader's Digest*, who get a steady flow of these stories in the mail, said that more than a hundred versions of the dead-battery tale came to them from at least a dozen States, and they still turn up at the magazine from time to time.

In most cases the narrator insists the story is God's own truth. Happened to their Cousin Herb.

■   ■

When Ed Wynn died one of the obituaries made a big point out of the assertion that the famous comic never uttered an off-color line in his whole career. I sometimes wonder why it is thought necessary to write such crap. I myself once heard Wynn tell his parrot story. He had a parrot, he said, that laid square eggs and could speak only one word. What was the word? Ouch!

■   ■

An aging farmer had gone along for several years without once acquiring an important though temporary manifestation that is considered essential if one is to make love to one's wife. Then one day he was out in the fields and God knows what thoughts were running through his mind, for suddenly it came upon him—the aforementioned manifestation.

Suspecting that it was a condition that might not endure for too long, he dropped everything and started running hard for the house. He took a straight line, hit a haystack and sent the hay a flying, collided with a cow and ran into the pump, but he scarcely slackened speed. He came roaring into the house, yelling to his wife to get ready, but she was a trifle slow in her preparations, pausing to put a dab of toilet water back of her ears, and by the time she *was* ready, his great urge had vanished.

A lapse of five years, and once again he was in the fields, and his wife was in the kitchen coring apples. She happened to glance out the window just in time to see her husband once again racing toward the house. He hit the corner of the barn and bounced off, and then whammed into the cow again, but he kept running toward the house, waving his arms wildly and yelling something at the top of his voice—she couldn't hear him but naturally she assumed he was howling for her to get ready. This time she was efficient. She dashed into her bedroom and flung off her clothes and had jumped onto the bed by the time he had entered the house. He rushed down the hall and past the bedroom door, but in passing he glanced in, and then he turned back and took one look at her, and cried out:

"My God, the house is on farr and this sex fiend wants to screw!"

■   ■

These two nubile maidens were having a heart-to-heart talk and Clarabelle was saying that when she got married she would know how to treat her man so that he would be contented, and happy that he had chosen her for his life's companion.

"I'd find out all the things he likes most to eat," she said, "and I'd learn to make them. Whenever he walked in the door from his job I'd already be in the kitchen fixing his favorite cocktail. I'd keep the house spotless, because that's the way a man likes it to be. I'd buy the kind of books he enjoys and I'd not neglect to invite his best friends to dinner from time to time. Now, Martha, what else could a man expect from a wife?"

"Nothing," said Martha, "unless he's got a dirty mind."

■   ■

The late Al Jolson was a raging hypochondriac, hence a great boon to the medical profession. Once on a social occasion one of Jolson's many doctors was telling him about a certain rare disease then under investigation.

"What makes this disease so odd," said the doctor, "is that the man who has it shows no outward sign of illness. In fact, he has no sensation of sickness at all—he looks and feels as if he were in perfect, robust health."

"My God!" cried Jolson, clutching at his chest. "*My* symptoms exactly!"

RECITATION NO. 6

(Transcription of a press conference with Lieut. Roger J. Rudder, American flying ace just returned from overseas duty in World War II; press conference supervised by Colonel Beaver of Air Force Public Relations.)

REPORTER: Welcome home, Lieutenant Rudder. How do you feel about being back in the States?

RUDDER: Pretty pissed off.

COLONEL BEAVER: Lieutenant Rudder's eyes were misty when the outlines of the Statue of Liberty, symbol of American faith and liberty, loomed into sight.

REPORTER: What is the first thing you plan to do in New York, Lieutenant?

RUDDER: Get laid.

COL. BEAVER: He intends to jet back to his old home town at once and see his Mom and all the folks.

REPORTER: Are they going to give you the Congressional Medal of Honor?

RUDDER: They damn well should.

COL. BEAVER: Lieutenant Rudder modestly shuns any high awards. "Every man in the battle line deserves it as much as I," he said.

REPORTER: What about the case of champagne General Geevil was going to send you for breaking Rickenbacker's record?

RUDDER: The old fart crapped out on me.

COL. BEAVER: Lieutenant Rudder is a teetotaler. At his suggestion the price of the champagne was happily donated to Russian relief.

REPORTER: Just how did you manage to shoot down so many enemy planes?

RUDDER: Because I'm a pretty frigging hot pilot.

COL. BEAVER: The Lieutenant attributes his enemy score to a combination of teamwork, luck, and superior equipment.

REPORTER: Do you think the German pilot is as good as the American?

RUDDER: I can fly circles up his ass.

COL. BEAVER: He pays high tribute to the skill of the enemy.

REPORTER: How about the Japs?

RUDDER: Those bastards don't know their butts from third base.

COL. BEAVER: What the Lieutenant means is that the quality of the Japanese airmen is declining somewhat.

REPORTER: Did you have a good American mechanic at hand?

RUDDER: Good? That dumb son of a bitch was born with his thumb up his rear end. It was a miracle that I ever got off the ground.

COL. BEAVER: Lieutenant Rudder is lavish in his praise of our courageous ground crews who worked round the clock to keep 'em flying.

REPORTER: We understand you intend to visit the factory where your plane was built.

RUDDER: That's right, if the bastards aren't out on strike. I'd like to get my hands on that horse's ass who welded his lunch bucket into the tail section of my ship.

COL. BEAVER: He is proud of our American workers and the magnificent way they are backing the attack.

REPORTER: I understand that you intend to teach some gunnery before you return to the wars.

RUDDER: Yeah. Somebody's gotta give the kids the ungarbled word. The stuff they taught me in training damn near got me my ass shot off.

COL. BEAVER: Rudder is unqualified in his praise of the excellent training being given our fledgling pilots.

REPORTER: Tell me, Lieutenant, does . . .

RUDDER: Sorry boys, that's enough. Gotta get outa here before the bars close and line up a piece of ass. So long.

COL. BEAVER: Yes, gentlemen, Lieutenant Rudder must now hurry along, to get back to his mother's apple pies, and the high school sweetheart he left behind, and the Main Street where he played cowboy-and-Indian as a boy. If there are any further questions, gentlemen, I believe I can field them. Fire away.

FUTZIN' AROUND
AT COOKING SCHOOL

I imagine most of you know about that rare character, ole Tennessee Ernie Ford. In my own estimate Ern would be a great man if he'd just hold down a little on the hymn-yelpin'. He is one of the real good storytellers of our time and nine seconds after prayin' a pea-pickin' prayer he's likely as not to light into one that would bring a blush to the cheeks of a coal-bucket. Here's one of Ern's I think you'll like.

Brother Semp, a pillar of the community, was gathered to his fathers and a large crowd turned out for the funeral in the town's little church. The preacher give a nice talk, and everybody cried adequate, and then the pallbearers put the casket on their shoulders and carried it down the path where the gate led into the graveyard. It happened that the corner of the casket bumped against the gatepost and a groan was heard inside. The men put the casket down at once and opened it and, sure enough, the old boy was still alive. They hustled him back home and got him into bed and began doctoring him, but it didn't do any good—a few days later he died again.

So they had another funeral. Same preacher with the same sorrowing words, same crowd weeping and wailing all over again. The pallbearers picked up the casket and started down the path to the graveyard again, with the people following along behind.

The casket was just about at the gate when somebody at the back of the line called out: "Watch out for that gatepost, boys!"

■   ■

Pamela Mason, who has a sharp cutting-edge to her tongue, the same being a gentle characteristic of the female of our species, began her television career as Tom Duggan's telephone girl. Mr. Duggan is not well known in the East but he has been quite famous from Chicago to Malibu for a long time. He has a sharp cutting-edge to his tongue. A telephone girl is a girl who sits off to one side and takes calls from the general public and passes questions along to the star of the show.

Pamela, being English, was not too well acquainted with American slang and so one evening during the show she called across to Mr. Duggan: "A gentleman wants to know if you are a fruit."

The studio people pointed to the door and said to Pamela, "Go." But sharp-tongued Mr. Duggan announced that if she went, he went, and so she stayed.

■   ■

A sister of mine was rummaging through some old papers the other day and she came upon a picture post card I had sent her twenty years ago from the Sheraton Bon Air in Augusta, Georgia. On the back I had written: "Met tourist camp prop. in S. C. Asked if he had a phone. He said, 'Shore, but you cain't hear on it.'"

■   ■

These two guys are walking along the street when they see an attractive young woman coming toward them. One of the boys leaves his friend's side, walks right up to the girl, and says, "Let's ——." She belts him a good one across the face and proceeds on her unspoiled way, and the rebuffed one rejoins his friend, who now says:

"Good God! What kind of a performance was that? *That's* no way to approach a girl!"

"What's wrong with it?"

"You *never* walk up to a girl, a strange girl, and say, 'Let's ——.' That's insane. There's got to be a little preliminary talk, sweet talk, soft talk, romantic talk. You've got to *romance* her a while before you proposition her."

"How do you mean, *romance* her?"

"Oh, you know. Talk to her about romantic things. Give her a line about soft romantic things."

"I don't know any soft romantic things," said the straight-forward fellow. "Give me a fer-instance."

"Well, talk to her about . . . oh, let's see . . . well, talk to her about the beauty of moonlight above the Mediterranean. That's one of the most romantic settings on earth. Talk to her about that. And then if . . ."

At this point another beautiful girl hove in view, and our Casanova again broke away and walked right up to her and said:

"Hey, kid. You ever seen the moon over the Mediterranean?"

"No," she said.

"Okay. Let's ——."

■　■

Sometimes when people ask me where the new humor writers are, meaning the people who write humor that is to be read, I say there are not many coming along—that the kids who have the talent come out of college or some other slum and go straight into television where the rewards are almost immediate and certainly much greater. I am speaking, of course, about money.

Agreed that there's an ever-swelling ocean of drivel on TV . . . there are also sparkling bits and lively lines coming out of the box from time to time. I think right now of two I heard recently. I don't have the names of the comics, but that's all right—the lines almost surely came from someone else.

"What worries me," said one fellow, "is that Tuesday Weld

may marry Hal March, Jr., and then she'll be Tuesday March the Second."

And another comic said *he* was bothered by the possibility of a bank merger in the Garden State. A bank in Red Bank, New Jersey, is absorbed by a bank in Long Branch, New Jersey, and people begin referring to "the Long Branch branch of the Red Bank bank."

■   ▪

The dialect in this next one will be slight and quite delicate, for it is Scottish. I have the same deep love for their way of talk as I have for their hideous God damned bagpipe music.

In his cottage on the south slopes of the Grampian Mountains old Kentigern lay dying. (There will be nobody named Sandy *or* MacTavish in this story.) Knowing that he was in his final hour he summoned his oldest friend, Bill Darnley.

"Bill," said old Kentigern.

"Yes, Bob," said old Darnley.

"I'm goin' fast, Bill, and a favor I want to ask of ye. You mind that bottle of Campbeltown whuskey I've been savin' all these long years, waitin' for the one big special occasion to drink it? That whusky, Bill, as you well know, is the finest of the fine and is now . . . let me see . . . a hundred and three years old. But I'm fadin' fast, Bill, and I won't be able to drink it, so after they get me in the ground, old friend, I want you to do something for me. Get the bottle out of yon cabinet and take it out to the cemetery and pour it all on my grave. Will ye do it, Bill? Will ye promise me?"

Bill stood for a few long moments in thought. Then he gave his answer.

"Of course, I'll do it, Bob. You know I'd do anything you ask, for you're my oldest and dearest friend. Just one favor, though, I'd like to ask of you. That beautiful whusky—would ye mind very much if, when I come to pour it on your grave, I run it just one time through me kidneys?"

■ ■

By crippled kayak and off-course catamaran out of Honolulu comes a Don Quinn story, relayed by Ed Sheehan who describes Brother Quinn quite accurately as one of the forever-greats of comedy writing. Mr. Quinn's latest tale concerns a photographer on the staff of a famous picture magazine, who is telling a colleague about a recent assignment in Central Park, as follows:

He was ambling along a pathway in the park when he encountered a dilapidated hag who braced him for coffee money. She was in rags, with stringy hair and busted shoes, but there was something about her suggesting a lost gentility. The cameraman got to talking with her and found that she had once been a wealthy socialite, with a town house and an estate in Connecticut, a fleet of Rolls Royces, a yacht, and buckets and buckets of jewels.

She told him that she had gone through a series of bad marriages with guys who had robbed her blind, and the stock market had not been kind to her and now, here she was, panhandling dimes—within sight of the white marble mansion where she had once reigned as queen. She was, indeed, a most pathetic character.

The second photographer shook his head sadly. "Real tough," he said, almost with a catch in his throat. "What did you give her?"

"Well," said the first photographer, "it was sort of a dark day so I gave her a 50th of a second at 4.5."

■ ■

Mention the word *jokebook* and the name of Joe Miller leaps into view. The name, in fact, has long been a synonym for a joke. For the benefit of those among you who are not acquainted with the facts of Joe Miller's life, I am now prepared to say that Joe Miller couldn't tell a joke with any skill at all, couldn't write a joke, had nothing whatever to do with the book that bore his name, and never even saw it. He was a comic actor with the Drury Lane company in London and his name was widely known for his work on stage. But it must be remembered that he was like many celebrated comics of our own time—almost always he spoke lines that were written by other men. It is ironic that he is designated as the author of the famous jokebook; he could neither read nor write. It was said that the only reason he got married was to have someone to read his parts to him so he could memorize them. This is not such an unusual state of affairs as it may seem at first glance. As I write this bit there are books on our best-seller lists bearing the names of people who are not far removed from Joe Miller's condition, "authors" who could not possibly write a note to the milkman and get it to parse.

The book, *Joe Miller's Jests,* was published a year after Miller's death. It was actually written by a destitute penny-a-liner named John Mottley, and Joe Miller's name was put on it because everyone in England knew who Joe Miller was, and knew that he had been a very funny man on the stage. The book business is as solid and granitic as Gibraltar, and never changes.

As is the case with almost all jokebooks, this eighteenth-century collection contains a few good ones and then, for filler, a great many crude, cruddy, stupid and senseless stories. The thing that interests me, in the main, is the vaunted "antiquity of jests" encountered in its pages. Here is a good example . . .

In 1967 there was published a fat biography of Harry Cohn, a powerhouse among motion picture producers and a son of a bitch of the first water, and second. The book was by Bob Thomas, and sold well, and many of the anecdotes contained in it were spread across the land. One of them attracted my attention. I had heard it before, possibly as applied to Harry Cohn, possibly about some other movie tycoon. I thought it was one of the best anecdotes I'd ever heard about the Hollywood Establishment, and I decided that it might be suitable material for use in my buskin'. So I wrote it, as follows:

One of my favorite Hollywood stories has been going the rounds again since publication of Bob Thomas's biography of Harry Cohn, for many years head of Columbia Pictures. His brother Jack ran the New York end of the business and once proposed to Harry that the studio turn out some biblical pictures. Jack pointed out that such pictures made big profits for DeMille and other producers.

"There are still," said Jack, "a lot of good stories in the Bible that haven't been used yet."

"What the hell do *you* know about the Bible?" Harry snorted.

"I know a lot about it," said Jack. "I've made it my business to look into it."

"I'll bet you don't even know the Lord's Prayer."

"How much?" demanded Jack.

"Fifty bucks." Each man posted the money and Harry ordered, "Okay, go ahead and say it."

Jack cleared his throat and began, "Now I lay me down to sleep, I pray . . ."

Harry scowled and shoved the money at his brother. "Hell," he said, "I didn't think you knew it."

As I mentioned, that joke was told widely on television and radio shows and I remember that Jack Paar used it when he did a TV special on the subject of Hollywood. So, about this time I arrived at the job of giving Joe Miller's book a thorough inspection. The original has been done in facsimile, in paperback, by Dover Publications at a buck per copy. The printing is in that oldtime kooky form where an "s" in a word becomes an "f" unless it is a terminal "s." It is fun to read for a while, where words are spelled: fuch, infifted, bufinefs, and fuchlike. Gets a little boring after a while. But anyway, on page 24 of Joe Miller we find this:

82. Two Gentlemen, difputing about Religion, in *Button's Coffee-Houfe,* faid one of them, I wonder, Sir, you fhoud talk of Religion, when I'll hold you five Guineas you can't fay the *Lord's Prayer,* done, faid the *other,* and Sir *Richard*

Steele fhall hold Stakes. The Money being depofited, the Gentleman began with, *I believe in God,* and fo went cleverly thro' the *Creed;* well, faid the other, I own I have loft; *I did not think he could have done it.*

(Them dumb bastards of the fplendid paft couldn't punctuate for four apples!)

I have encountered several other jests in Joe Miller that are told and printed today and attributed to living people, but the Harry Cohn bit will suffice to illustrate the point. I am not being critical of Mr. Thomas—I'm quite sure that I, myself, on more than one occasion, have been snared by the same delusion.

As I remarked earlier, there are some good stories in Joe Miller, so let us try a few without the trick spelling and daffy punctuation.

■　■

5. When the Duke of Ormond was young and came first to Court he happened to stand next my Lady Dorchester, one evening in the drawing-room, who being but little upon the reserve on most occasions, let a fart, upon which he looked her full in the face and laughed. "What's the matter, my Lord?" said she. "Oh, I heard it, madam," replied the Duke. "You'll make a fine courtier, indeed," said she, "if you mind every thing you *hear* in this place."

24. The great Algernon Sidney seemed to show as little concern at his death, he had indeed got some friends to intercede with the King for a pardon; but when he was told that His Majesty could not be prevailed upon to give him his life, but that in regard to his ancient and noble family, he would remit part of his sentence, and only have his *head* cut off; "Nay," said he, "if His Majesty is resolved to have my *head,* he may make a whistle of my *ass* if he pleases."

25. Lady C. and her two daughters having taken lodgings at the Sign of the Cock and Leather-Breeches in Piccadilly, was always put to the blush when she was obliged to give anybody

directions to her lodgings, the sign being so odd a one; upon which milady, sending for her landlord, told him she liked him and his lodgings very well but she must be obliged to quit them on account of his sign. "Oh, dear Madam," said the young fellow, "I would do anything rather than lose such good lodgers—I can alter my sign." "So I think," answered milady, "and I'll tell you how you may satisfy both me and my daughters: only take down your *breeches* and let your *cock* stand."

153. A gentleman said of a young wench who constantly plyed about the Temple, that if she had as much law in her *head,* as she had had in her *tail,* she would be one of the ablest counsel in England.

203. An Irishman whom King Charles II had some esteem for, one day coming into the King's presence, His Majesty asked him how his wife did, who had just been cut for a fistula in her backside. "I humbly thank Your Majesty," replied Teague, "She's like to do well, but the Surgeon says, it will be an eye-sore as long as she lives."

■   ■

Quickly, let me say: them Englishmen never really change. There was this London fellow who was in the business of organizing African safaris. A prospective customer asked him if it were true that sometimes a rhinoceros would come charging down on a safari-car. "Yes," said the promoter, "but it's a practice to be frowned on."

■   ■

In the years when Hollywood was the movie capital of the world it was my pleasure to work there off and on and to observe at close range the people inhabiting the city which Rufus Blair always called Double Dubuque. Yet I never did get to see one of the greatest performances in the history of the theatrical arts—Eddie Sutherland reciting *Incident of the French Camp* by Robert Browning.

Sutherland's career paralleled that of Chaplin and, in fact, he worked for Chaplin for a long time. He was a graduate of the English music halls and was one of the most agile of the old Keystone cops. It was said that Eddie Sutherland could execute a pratfall of such violent beauty that it took the breath away from the onlooker. Later he gave up acting and became one of the industry's top directors.

On social occasions Sutherland the Director was quiet and dignified and few people who didn't know him ever suspected that he had been a star of the slapstick days. And so it was, at Hollywood parties, the host would conspire with Eddie and ask him to recite *Incident of the French Camp*. "You always do it so well," the host would say, and Eddie would blush and bridle, not wanting to recite, but the host would wheedle and cajole and the guests would squirm because, most certainly, *they* didn't want to hear any goddam pomes recited out no matter if Robert L. Service.

And so, solemnly and melodramatically, Sutherland would launch into the recital about the boy soldier bringing the tidings of Ratisbon to Bonaparte, standing on a little mound a mile or so from the battle. Sutherland built it . . . and he *was* the boy soldier as he spoke the final lines:

> "You're wounded!" "Nay," his soldier's pride
> Touched to the quick, he said:
> "I'm killed, sire!" and his chief beside;
> Smiling the boy fell dead.

As he uttered that last line, Eddie Sutherland let a sickly smile play across his lips and then took off—leaping three or four feet into the air and then hitting the floor with a horrendous crash, a fall sufficient to maim an ordinary man for life. But after a half minute of playing dead, he was back on his feet, as good as new and ready for a drink. I consider it a sin of chronological injustice that Robert Browning could not have seen the Sutherland recitation.

■ ■

Heard a fella tell this one on the NBC radio today. Plain out. Shows the way things have gone. This little girl was always sucking her thumb and her mother finally told her, "If you don't quit doing that you're going to swell up and bust." A few days later a friend of the mother, a lady who was pregnant beyond all reason, came for a visit. The little girl stared at her swollen middle and exclaimed: "I know what *you* been doin'!"

■ ■

I have never met David Raskin but I admire him for the two things I know about him. The first is the fact that he collaborated with Johnny Mercer on the splendid song, "Laura." The second is a thing he said about the motion picture "Lifeboat" during the time it was being produced at Twentieth Century-Fox.

One noontime in the studio commissary a couple of screenwriters were ragging Mr. Raskin about the unimportance of his work. They told him that the great Alfred Hitchcock had decided there would be no music in his new picture.

"Why?" asked Mr. Raskin.

"The whole picture takes place in a lifeboat, out in the middle of the ocean, and Hitchcock is being logical—there couldn't *be* any music out there. Where could it possibly come from?"

"I'd like to suggest," said Mr. Raskin, "that you go ask Mr. Hitchcock where his *cameras* come from out in the middle of the ocean, and I'll tell him where the music comes from."

■ ■

Shortly after I arrived in New York in 1929 and found work as a reporter, I attended a small luncheon in honor of H. G. Wells. I boldly chiseled my way into a chair two seats removed from the great man. I sat in rapt silence, scarcely daring to lift a fork for fear I would miss a few words of his casual discourse. All through that luncheon he spoke of only one thing. He said he didn't like green peas; he added that he could not remember ever having liked green peas, and before the meal was finished he asserted that he was confident he would go to his grave disliking green peas.

■ ■

I know a journalist in Texas, where the word *journalist* is an execration, by the name of Hart Stilwell, a man of various talents and insights. Everything that Stilwell writes is God's truth, to hear him tell it, this being a general characteristic of journalists everywhere. So we must believe the Scissors Story, because Stilwell tells it and Stilwell says it is true.

A sensitive farmer had some scrubby acres along the Brazos River and he had, also, a wife who nagged him on a single subject: scissors. She wanted a pair of scissors. Every day of her life, often more than once, she'd whine about scissors. And after a while her husband got so fed up with it that he promised himself he'd *never*, in this world or the next, get her any scissors. Still, she kept up the nagging and eventually the time came when he began to threaten her. Again and again he warned her to quit mentioning the word *scissors* in his presence, and she never faltered, so finally he started telling her that if she didn't stop he'd knock her brains out. Her answer was, "I sure need me a pair uh scissors."

One day the farmer and his wife were picking berries along the river bank and she began wondering to herself, aloud, how it would work if she had a pair of scissors to cut the berry stems. Her husband blew a gasket. He told her that if he ever heard her employ the word *scissors* again he would kill her.

Five minutes later she tore a long rip in her dress, which got caught in the brambles, and she said, "My! I could go right up to the house and fix this rip so's nobody would ever know it, per-vided I had me a pair of scissors."

Her husband let out a bellow of rage, grabbed her, and threw her into the river. With deep satisfaction he stood on the bank to watch her drown. She went down once, and came up. She went down a second time, and surfaced. And just as she was going down for the third and last time, she held her right hand straight up above her head with the middle and index fingers extended, so that those fingers were the last part of her to be seen, and they were moving slowly, like the blades of a pair of scissors.

■　　■

A dozen years back I had a letter from Walter Davenport, one of the top men in American magazine-writing. Mr. Davenport told me that a report had just reached him to the effect that Jim Bishop was scurrying around the Holy Land doing some "original research" on the Crucifixion. "According to my informant," Mr. Davenport wrote, "Bishop has found out that Christ had a cocker spaniel."

Walter Davenport was the reporter who was fired from the New York *Journal* by Gene Fowler, who rarely ever fired anyone. Davenport was covering a suffragette parade and described the grand marshal as riding a "dappled-gray" horse. Fowler, it happened, knew that the horse was pure white, and canned Davenport. He was reinstated, however, when he came into the office and explained that he had covered the parade through a saloon window which was covered with fly specks.

RECITATION NO. 7

Confederate Memo to The Brotherhood:

Our correspondent in the Piedmont tobaccolands has just sent me a report on the latest juridical developments in the town of Haggs Corner. The name of the town is made up, but the incident reported is true in every detail.

A young man of the town was charged with rape, the girl being a member of an old and well-to-do family. The case came to trial with a jury of twelve men. The defense attorney made it clear from the beginning that he intended to charge the girl with responsibility, contending that she provoked the boy into this most reprehensible act.

In his summation to the jury, the defense lawyer played his theme long and loud. He spoke to the men of the jury, using this thought over and over: "What would *you* do, if a pretty and shapely young girl came at you, and swarmed over you, and kissed you on the neck and shoulders, and flung her arms around you, and pulled you to her breast? I ask you, gentlemen, what would *you* have done?"

At about this stage of the proceedings defense counsel took note of an elderly juror, with handlebar mustaches, seated in the middle of the box, and this old guy was beginning to strain forward a trifle, and his eyes were bugging out ever so slightly. Defense counsel decided to concentrate his fire on this man. He stared straight into the old gent's eyes and continued: "I ask you, what would *you* have done if this beautiful young girl had slipped out of her dress, and if she had taken hold of your hand and placed it inside her brassiere? What would *you* have done?" Still talking straight at old handlebars. "What would *you* have done, if this selfsame young girl had taken hold of you and pulled you down on top of her . . ." The old man was about to leap out of the jury box . . . "and then had thrown her arms around you, and reached down to pull open the zipper of your trousers? I ask you, what would *you* have done?"

The old man, now leaning far forward, answered loud and clear:

"Ah'd uh screwed 'er!"

Mistrial, and the case had to be transferred to another county.

YOCKING IT UP
AT THE INSTITUTE
FOR ADVANCED STUDY

If someone will be so kind as to insinuate a hippopotamus into this conversation, I will manage to overhear it and it will remind me of a story I know about a hippopotamus.

There *are* people who will stubborn up and refuse to tell a story because they are not *reminded* of it. I imagine that everyone present has heard of Lord Chesterfield, the man who wrote those letters to his son. Few people know much *about* him. He was a horse's ass of the first water. He did, however, touch upon the subject I've been discussing here—the matter of being *reminded* of a story. Listen to the horse's ass Lord Chesterfield:

> I knew a man who had a story about a gun, which he thought a good one and that he told it very well. He tried all means in the world to turn the conversation upon guns; but, if he failed in his attempt, he started in his chair, and said he heard a gun fired; but when the company assured him they heard no such thing, he answered, perhaps then I was mistaken; but, however, since we are talking of guns—and then told his story, to the great indignation of the company.

Lord Chesterfield was, in addition, a bum writer. Hark! Did I hear someone mention the hippopotamus? Makes me think of a story about a movie producer in Hollywood whose studio assigned him to do a jungle picture. This producer had all of the qualities of Lord Chesterfield, and then some. This jungle picture was to be a "B-minus" film, but never to him. He called a meeting of his underlings.

"Now, get this," he said. "I'm gonna do this jungle picture and it's gonna be the biggest, the greatest jungle picture in history. Everything about it is gonna be great. It's gonna have everything —the most tigers, the most lions, the most zebras, the most elephants. And a hippopotamus. Fellas, this picture is gonna have the biggest hippopotamus in the world in it."

A writer broke in: "Where do you expect to get it?"

"I should worry my head about such things! When I say I want the biggest hippopotamus in the world, I want the biggest God damn hippopotamus in *history*. Now *you* tell *me* where we get it."

They put the research department to work on the problem. In a surprisingly short while the producer was notified that the biggest hippopotamus in the world, at least the biggest hippopotamus in captivity, was the property of the London Zoo.

"Buy the son of a bitch!" ordered the dynamic producer, and negotiations were opened by cable. After a while a price, something on the order of $50,000, was agreed upon and the question of transportation arose. The London Zoo people urged that the buyer engage the services of the two regular hippopotamus keepers—men who knew how to handle the beast.

"How much salary?" the studio cabled London. The two men could be hired for fifty dollars a week. Please keep in mind that all this occurred back in Pleistocene times when I worked in a Hollywood studio.

"No!" roared the producer. He was willing to spend $50,000 for the hippo but he balked at fifty dollars a head for people. "We got people in this studio," he said, "who can handle any animal on earth. Why pay them guys?"

Two men from the prop department were shipped off to London with instructions to bring back the hippo. They got him on a ship and then they got him off the ship and into a special freight car. In due course the freight car arrived in Los Angeles. The problem now was to get the hippopotamus out of the freight car and into the movie jungle. The hippo wouldn't cooperate.

"He won't cooperate," they told the producer. This phrase is a common one around the studios. It is almost the nastiest thing that can be said, whether applied to a hippopotamus or a human being.

"Drag the bastard out of it," ordered the producer.

They ripped off the upper structure of the freight car, leaving the hippo sprawled in full view. They built runways, but the hippo spurned them. He was a sick hippopotamus. He was out of his element. Those men from the prop department were geniuses when it came to handling period furniture and tomahawks and Congress gaiters, but they knew little about the mental processes of a hippopotamus.

After hours of wrestling with the problem they hired the biggest flat-bed truck they could find and backed it up to the railroad car. They brought in a powerful crane and a barrel or two of grease. They fastened chains around the recumbent invalid and they *drug* him off. They drug him onto the truck and drove him to the place where the jungle had been built. Now a new problem arose. The hippopotamus was prone to stay prone. They didn't want to drag him off the truck and onto the ground for fear they would injure him. Then along came someone with a thought bordering on intelligence.

"That hippopotamus is sick as a dog," he said. "He has got to be up to his chin in water. An animal like that sops up water through his pores. He's been away from water so long he's a nervous wreck."

Everyone agreed that he should be put in water for a while. But where? Someone remembered a small lake not too far from Hollywood.

"Lease the lake," ordered the producer, "and dump the bastard in."

They leased the lake. They drove the truckload of hippopotamus to the shore. He showed no interest in the water. They didn't want to roll him off into shallow water for fear he'd founder in the mud and never get loose. So they summoned an army of

110

studio carpenters and quickly built a stout pier extending out to deep water. When the pier was finished and tested they backed the truck onto it. Next they brought up a hoisting engine. They blocked the rear wheels of the truck securely, attached a line to the front of the truck, and slowly tilted it upward. At an angle of around forty-five degrees the hulk of hippopotamus began to move. The great beast slid slowly off the tilted truck, then hit the water with a prodigious splash. The job had been done neatly and without a hitch, and a great cheer went up among the workmen on shore.

The animal went under water at once and silence settled over the spectators as they waited for his happy reappearance. The seconds ticked off and nothing happened. More seconds, and still nothing.

The biggest God damn hippopotamus in the world hasn't come up to this day.

■　■

Again out of deepest Mexico comes a tale from Paul Perez, the retired screenplay carpenter. Paul tells of a female relative who drove a staff car in the Royal Air Force during World War II. One day she chauffeured a Brigadier to a new installation in the country and later the two stayed on for dinner. It was late in the evening when they started back for London. Soon they were going through a dark wood and the girl slowed the car and spoke over her shoulder:

"Would the Brigadier mind if I got out and spent a penny?" This being English-English for go-to-the-bathroom. The Brigadier said: "How thoughtless of me, my child, not to realize that an Air Force installation would not have facilities for young women. Go right ahead, and take as long as you wish." So she got out and made her way some distance into the wood and spent her penny (she may even have squandered it) and then hurried back to the car and drove home to London. Pulling up in front of Air Force HQ in Trafalgar Square she got out and opened the rear door and stood smartly at attention, but no Brigadier came out.

Back yonder in the woods . . . he, too, had got out to spend a penny of his own.

■   ■

The Australian sense of fun is closer to the American than to the English. They play around with jokes that have been in circulation in the United States for a long time.

Two Australian migratory workers were tramping across country when one took his pipe out of his mouth and pointing with the stem, said, "Nice wheat."

The other one didn't answer. No more was said for five hours when they had made camp and were preparing for bed. The second man then said, " 'Twas oats," and rolled into his blanket and went to sleep. When he awoke the next morning his pal was gone, and there was a note under a rock, saying: "Goin. Too bloody much argyment."

■   ■

In North Carolina many citizens are engaged in the manufacture and sale of furniture, and so furniture stories are plentiful. An old reliable concerns the lady from the hill country who went into the furniture store and asked for a sexual sofa. The salesman puzzled over this one a moment, then said, "You must mean a *sectional* sofa."

"Sexual, sectional," she replied, "I don't know which, all I know is I'm lookin' for an occasional piece in the livin' room."

■   ■

Which brings us again to the ever-fascinating subject of Confederate-type talk. My sister Rita met a colored woman on the street in Richmond one day, a woman who was a cook employed in the home of a friend.

"Susie," said Rita, "I'll never forget the apple pie you made the last time I was over. Would you tell me what you put in it to make it so good."

"Nothin' to it, honey," said Susie. "I jist flavors it up with nutneg, sinnina, an' sooger."

And in the same city two gentlemen had finished lunch at a counter and noted that two checks had been placed nearby, one obviously belonging to a lady on an adjoining stool. They summoned the waiter who picked out one of the checks and shoved it toward the gentlemen.

Said the waiter: "This un's yallzun's."

■   ■

If you people think it is strange that I am not joining you at the flowing bowl this time, just consider that I am being eccentric and consider, also, that long ago I passed my quota. I have had my share of the happy waters, and a tank car or two above it. It is probable that I have had traffic with potables that you've never heard of.

The Fitzroy cocktail, for example. Not long ago I was in Sydney, Australia, and I had my first and only Fitzroy cocktail at the home of a newspaper editor. It is a drink favored in the outback country and its composition is as follows: equal parts of methylated spirits and ginger beer, then stir in one teaspoon of boot polish.

It's delectable, and causes your neckbones to crack loudly.

Once in Rapid City, South Dakota, a man named Ingvalson served me a heady beverage which he described as genuine Indian-trader whisky. It was a brand of booze invented by early traders who found it to be of great value, for one cupful of it was sufficient to drive an Indian clean out of his mind. Hence, said this Mr. Ingvalson, it was a whisky quite adequate for intimate little social affairs in the modern American home. I still have the notebook in which I scrawled the prescription and as near as I can translate it, here it is:

Slosh two gallons raw alcohol into one barrel Missouri River water. Add two ounces strychnine to drive the drinker slightly crazy and then put in three plugs of eatin' tobacco and let it marinate a few days to make the Indian sick—an Indian wouldn't figure it was whisky unless it made him horribly sick. Put in five bars of soap to give it a nice bead, a half pound of Mexican chili peppers, some sage brush, and then boil this until it is a nice brown.

I've never made it in my own home. Too much trouble getting the water.

■ ■

Ernie Rogers, the perceptive newspaper columnist who became Mayor of Upper Peachtree Street in Atlanta, was sitting with a group of Georgia gentlemen when the conversation touched on popular songs.

Among the company was one soigné Cracker of the type known to mankind as a Wise Guy.

"For my money," he declared in his customary *ex cathedra* tone, "the greatest popular song of them all was written by Hoagy Carmichael."

Another member in the group interrupted: "You mean the guy Samuel Goldwyn called Hugo Carmichael? Which song did you have in mind?"

The Goldwynism must have thrown the pontifical one, for he responded:

"Sawdust."

■ ■

Once upon a time I wrote a piece in the *Saturday Evening Post* based on the practice of wheedling free advice out of doctors, lawyers and other professional men. Since then I have heard of a man who reigned as champion in this field—the Broadway producer, Max Gordon. The story goes that Mr. Gordon never passed up an opportunity to pick up some free information.

In New Deal days he was invited to lunch at the White House by Eleanor Roosevelt and before sitting down Gordon was introduced to another guest, a Doctor So-and-so. Gordon didn't waste a second. "Doctor," he said, "I hate to bother you but sometimes after I've eaten I feel these pains right along in here . . ."

The doctor interrupted him. "I'm not a physician, Mr. Gordon," he smiled. "I'm a doctor of economics."

"So," Max Gordon came back at him lightning-like, "so what's good in the market, Doc?"

■　■

Hold still briefly, friends, for another doctor item. On a Sunday afternoon this Chappaqua physician took down with a beastly affliction—a stopped-up toilet. He tried his hand at the task of fixing it, only to create greater havoc, and then he called his plumber, who had been a patient of his for years.

He told the plumber the nature of his difficulty. "It's messed up half the house," he said, "and I wish you'd hop in your car and get right over here and do something about it."

"Sorry, Doc, but I can't make it," said the plumber. "Tell you what you do. Just drop a couple of aspirins in it and I'll stop by first thing in the morning."

■　■

And that last line—well, it's peculiar how one leads right into another. This Southern lady called the cops one evening and said that a man had busted into her home and was raping her. Was he there now? Sure. How long had he been there?

"He been here about two hours," she said, "and I want you to send some offisuhs over here on the double . . . fust thing to-morrow mawnin'."

■　■

Oscar Levant, who withholds very little from the public, has written about an encounter he once had with a Chicago gangster named Greasythumb Guzik. Levant made the acquaintance of Guzik and another mobster on a train, and they told Oscar about a gangster convention they had attended recently in Chicago. One of the choice bits of convention entertainment, they said, came when one of the delegates cheerfully laid a broad in the presence of the assembled hoods.

"Five times without withdrawal!" Greasythumb announced—proudly, as if it had been himself.

Levant said he was properly awed by this statistic and later on told his wife about it.

"Just how did they know?" she demanded.

■ ■

I don't know if black comedy and sick humor are the same, but they may amalgamate in this: a Negro comic was asked, on a television show, if he had been punished when he was a child.

"Oh, no," he said. "Just cautioned a little. I can remember one day when my Mama beat me with a cat-o'-nine-tails. The ends of the leather strings had been dipped in concrete, to make see-ment knots. She beat me till I lay bleeding on the floor and she herself sunk to her knees, tears running down her cheeks, and she looked at me in her motherly way and cried out, 'You just wait tell yo' PAPA gits home!'"

■ ■

It would please me to have an even one thousand years of life after death so I might catch up on the books I want to read and haven't had time for in my present peculiar incarnation. For one thing I'd like to spend a few years getting better acquainted with the work of Charles Lamb. Just the other day I read a sentence of his: "Nothing puzzles me more than time and space; and yet nothing puzzles me less, for I never think about them." As the farmer said, that guy thinks just like me.

One thing of Lamb's I know about, is A Dissertation on Roast Pig. I know also that the basic idea for the tale was borrowed by some American writer, quite a few years back, for use in a fable concerned with the origin of Bourbon whisky. I haven't been able to trace the story, nor has Mr. Emil A. Pavone of the Bourbon Institute, though we agree that it sounds as if it might have been the work of Irvin S. Cobb.

The tale goes that in former times, in Bourbon County, the corn mash was distilled into plain corn whisky. During one good year a certain Orville Moody had so much of the stuff in barrels that his shed wouldn't hold it all so he rolled one barrel out and stood it near a big oak tree. Some days later, during a storm, a bolt of lightning grazed the barrel, splintering it across the top but doing no harm to the staves. Orville Moody figured that part of his supply was spoiled and the barrel just stood there until winter was coming on. One day Orville decided to dump the faulty barrel and he was rolling it to the edge of the woods when some of the liquid splashed out on his hand, and he put his tongue to it, and then he ran for the house and got a dipper, and drank some of it. After that he called in some of his neighbors to taste it, and they exclaimed over it, and for a while no one could figure out why this particular barrel should contain such nectar. At last they puzzled it out—the lightning had charred the inside surfaces of the barrel staves and that charred wood had given the special heavenly taste to plain ordinary cawn.

From that day forward, according to the story, whenever an electrical storm arrived, the mountaineers all over the neighborhood could be seen feverishly rolling their barrels of whisky out of their sheds and standing them under the trees.

■ ■

Back in the 1930s two of the top movie stars in Hollywood got married in what was proclaimed to be The Wedding of the Year. Both parties were towering figures in romantic photoplays, and had sex, and their wedding was an event of about the same splendor as a British coronation wingding.

When their first anniversary was approaching they were still somehow living together and the famous young husband decided that he would pretend to forget the date. Then he went about the business of organizing a surprise party for his beautiful bride. It would be held in the big house they occupied in the San Fernando Valley.

The young husband planned the surprise party for late afternoon and then managed to arrange for his wife to go horsebacking that day. He invited a couple of hundred prominent members of the film colony and gave each guest written instructions about parking cars several blocks away from the house.

The afternoon came, the lady went riding, and now the guests began arriving. They were ushered through the big central hall-way and then led into the adjoining drawing room, and the library, and the heavy doors closed upon them.

Into the house, finally, came the unsuspecting lady. She waved a gay greeting to her husband as she went tripping up the broad staircase, and he could hear her humming a song aloft in her boudoir. Carefully he opened the doors and out of the library and the drawing room tiptoed the guests. There was much shushing and fingers-to-lips and then they were all in position, all standing in a crowd in the big hallway. The moment had come for the husband to call up to his wife and summon her downstairs. But before he could do it, her own voice rang out from the upper floor:

"Bay-bee! I've got my panties off now if you want some yum-yum!"

■   ■

A young man with a prosperous clothing business in the New York garment district had just been congratulating himself, in his office, for being so fortunate—a thriving business, a beautiful wife, and a handsome baby boy. The telephone rang. It was the beautiful wife and she was breathless in her excitement.

"Dolling!" she cried. "The baby has spoken his first words! Three of them!"

"Whad he say?" cried her husband.

"Momma, poppa, and gabardine!"

■   ■

These two black-whiskered old guys were sitting on a stoop on New York's Lower East Side, feeling the warmth of the sun and indulging themselves in idle talk. One was a native of Minsk in the old country, and the other came from Pinsk.

These two enjoyed disputation, and often went out of their way to get into arguments.

This day the old man from Pinsk abruptly made a firm and unequivocal statement: "No good Jew ever comming from Minsk."

"That," spoke up his friend, "I'm challenging with every bun in mine boddy! Planty good Jews comming from Minsk!"

"None!" proclaimed the man from Pinsk. "Never wan good Jew from Minsk!"

"All kines!" insisted his friend. "Plannnnnty good Jews from Minsk!"

"Name one!"

The old man from Minsk tilted his head back and began thinking. He cocked his head to one side and pulled at his ear and wrapped himself in deep thought. He lowered his head and ran his fingers through his whiskers and went ummmmmm-ummmmmmm-ummmmmmm, thinking hard. He cupped his hand over his mouth and squinched up his eyes and thought almost furiously. At last he raised his head and asked:

"This Jew, does he *gotta* be from Minsk?"

■   ▫

George Oppenheimer, the drama critic, remembers the story of the glamorous actress who made a date with a young actor to spend the evening together at her apartment. At the last minute she found she had to go to a studio and have some photographs taken so she handed her date the key to her apartment.

"Let yourself in, darling," she said. "You'll find drinks on the sideboard. Help yourself, make yourself at home, play the radio, go in the bedroom, get undressed and if I'm not there start without me."

▨   ■

Mr. Oppenheimer also tells of the time he was taking his physical before induction into the Air Force. He was to be a member of a Motion Picture Unit and during the course of his physical furnished a specimen of urine. The bottle was picked up by a private first class, who was a dedicated movie fan. He placed it on a tray and then pointed to another bottle nearby, and whispered reverently, "Cary Grant."

■　■

As near as I can make out, the following story is authentic Dorothy Parker. One night Mrs. Parker gave a party for some of the old Algonquin Hotel gang and along about midnight into the room came a tornado in the person of Tallulah Bankhead. Miss Bankhead had but recently come up from Alabama to conquer the New York stage and now, after some hard times, she was well on her way. She had been in two successive hits and established herself and this night she was celebrating.

Until Tallulah arrived the Parker party had been fairly circumspect, but Miss Bankhead was in great spirits. She leaped about the room and did splits and kissed all the gentlemen and started throwing bottles around and committed a couple of handsprings and otherwise gave vent to her good feeling. Finally a committee of four gentlemen escorted her from the room and as things began to quiet down the hostess, Mrs. Parker, peeped through the curtains of an adjoining room and inquired in a timid voice:

"Has Whistler's Mother left yet?"

■　■

Jim Bridger was one of the fabled Mountain Men of our pioneer West. Once he was guiding an exploration party across the Rockies when one of the men managed to cut a deep gash in his leg. Jim took care of binding it up and reassured the victim: "Don't worry none about it ketchin' a infection—meat always keeps good in the mountains."

■　■

William Jennings Bryan was campaigning in the West and his train stopped at a hamlet where a crowd of farmers had assembled to hear him orate. Bryan got off the train and looked around for a speakers' stand but nobody had thought to put one up, and his eye fell on an old manure-spreader standing near the tracks.

Without hesitation Bryan climbed upon this vehicle, faced his audience, and began: "This is the first time I ever delivered a speech while standing on the Republican platform."

Sixty years later a story was being told of a visit by Hubert Humphrey to the Lyndon B. Johnson ranch for a conference on campaign strategy. Johnson and Humphrey were walking in the fields when the candidate for the vice-presidency accidentally put his foot into a cow flop.

"Mr. President," said Humphrey, "I just stepped on the Republican platform."

Moral, if any: Democratic politicians are more earthy.

■　■

That salty old General of World War II, Joseph W. Stilwell, had a personal motto: *Illegitimati non Carborundum.* His own translation of it: Don't let the bastards grind you down.

■　■

There was a gentleman's club in Richmond where the quality of the whisky was high, especially when it came to Bourbon. It was a matter of great pride among the members that they knew good Bourbon when they tasted it and there were a few who considered themselves as infallible in this department. One such was General Coates.

Came that cataclysmic day when, standing in elegance at the bar, the General announced that he had just been served Bourbon that was inferior, that was bad, that couldn't qualify as sheepdip.

"This bubbon," he declaimed, elevating the hateful tumbler, "this heah bubbon is im-bued with a strong flavuh of metal— some kinda *ahn*, Ah should say—and moah than that, a strong flavuh of leathuh."

These astonishing declarations brought other members to the bar and there was much excited talk, and in support of his allegations General Coates urged his cronies to have a taste of the whisky in the bottle that stood before him. None of the others could detect a taste of iron or leather. The General sipped again and said by gad he was right. He declared that he was the best

God damn judge of Bourbon in all Virginia and he knew what he was talking about. He called for other bottles of the same brand of Bourbon and had them opened and tasted them and in the end, he announced that only the whisky in that single bottle had the taste of iron and leather. By now his friends were beginning to needle him, and he grew angry, and said that no matter what the cost, he would prove his point.

He got on a train and went up to Kentucky and to the distillery where the Bourbon had been bottled. He stated his case to the head of the distillery who said politely that the General was laboring under a heavy delusion. But General Coates stuck to his guns and asked to have a look at the plant. He arrived finally in a great room where there were a dozen or more large vats containing whisky. He was told that this was the point in production where the Bourbon was ready for bottling.

He asked for a teaspoon. He moved from vat to vat, and tasted, and at last his expression changed and he cried out, "This is it!"

He now requested that the whisky in this particular vat be drained out carefully, and there was an objection, but he said he would happily pay for the cost of the operation. And so a siphon was put to work and the Bourbon drained out, with the General and the head of the distillery standing by, nervous and sweating.

Came the moment when the hose was making its last gugglings on the bottom of the vat, and the General was leaning in, searching with his eyes, and then he uttered a cry of triumph, and eagerly climbed over the wall of the vat and snatched a small object from the bottom and held it aloft. It was a tiny square of leather with a carpet tack through it.

■   ■

A few of my dearest friends may possibly remember that I once wrote a book about London and its environs. In the course of that narrative I took to discussing that remarkable man Sir Walter Raleigh, who is known nowadays as a character in a beautiful comedy sketch written and performed by Bob Newhart.

I made mention of Sir Walter's way with the ladies, and I

quoted a paragraph from the works of John Aubrey, a seven-teenth-century antiquary. The paragraph goes:

> He loved a wench well; and one time getting up one of the Mayds of Honour against a tree in a Wood ('twas his first lady), who seemed at first to be something fearfull of her Honour, and modest, she cryed, Sweet Sir Walter, what doe you me ask? Will you undoe me? Nay, sweet Sir Walter! Sweet Sir Walter! Sir Walter! . . . Swisser Swatter! Swisser Swatter!

After my book was published a lady in Illinois wrote me that she thought that paragraph was the best thing in it. She was so impressed by it, she went on, that she had set herself the task of digging out and reading the entire written works of John Aubrey. Which is much more than I have done. Swisser Swatter!

RECITATION NO. 8

(Whilst about two sheets in the wind, Sidney B. Whipple sometimes recited the following New England bit. Unfortunately I never copied it down and this version comes from a couple of other sources, plus my own memory.)

We was cruisin' down the Mozambique Channel under reefed tops'ls and the wind blowin' more'n half a gale, two years outer New Bedford and no ile. And the masthead lookout shouts, "Thar she blows!" And Mr. Sewell goes aft.

"Cap'n Hubbard," says he, "the man says 'Thar she blows!' Shall I laower away?"

"Mr. Sewell," says the cap'n, "it's weatherin' a little too peart and I don't see fitten fer to laower." So Mr. Sewell goes forrard.

Then the man at the masthead sings out, "Thar she blows and breaches!" And Mr. Sewell goes aft.

"Cap'n Hubbard," says he, "the man at the masthead says, 'Thar she blows and breaches!' Shall I laower away?"

"Mr. Sewell," says the cap'n, "it's a-blowin' too peart and I don't see fitten to laower." And Mr. Sewell goes forrard.

The lookout at the masthead sings out, "Thar she blows and breaches, and sparm at that!" And Mr. Sewell goes aft.

"Cap'n Hubbard," says he, "the man says, 'Thar she blows and breaches, and sparm at that!' Shall I laower away?"

"Mr. Sewell," says the cap'n, "it's a-blowin' too peart and I don't see fitten fer to laower, but if so be it that you sees fitten fer to laower, Mr. Sewell, why laower away and be good and God damned to ye."

And Mr. Sewell lowers and we goes on the whale, and Mr. Sewell is hell on the long dart, and when we comes in a hundred foot of her he says, "Put me jest three seas closeter, fer I'm hell on the long dart." And he slammed the iron and it tuk.

When we come alongside the ship, Cap'n Hubbard stands in the gangway. "Mr. Sewell," sez he, "you are the finest mate that ever sailed this ship, and you sartinly are hell on the long dart. Below in the locker on the port side there's rum and seegars at your sarvice."

"Cap'n Hubbard," says he, "I don't want your rum, no more your seegars. All I want of you is a little plain see-vility, and that of the commonest God damnedest kind."

HONEYFUGGLING AT
A STRAWBERRY FESTIVAL

A lot of the stories I know are concerned with the book-publishing business and many of them would be of interest only to other people involved in that business. I think of one, however, that may have a sort of universal appeal. It is about a famous book publisher whom I shall call Mr. Cartwright. He drank.

Mr. Cartwright lived in a town some distance from his business in New York City, and this town had a history dating back to the American Revolution. There had been a notable battle, or rendezvous, or encampment, on the edge of the town, and now the people of the community were getting up a big celebration of the anniversary. Leading residents were going to participate in a re-enactment of the battle or skirmish, and some were to take the parts of leading actors in the drama. The committee chose Mr. Cartwright to play the role of General Lafayette. He and George Washington were to be mounted on horses, side by side, as the historical pageant unfolded, and that was all they had to do— except maybe throw a salute now and then.

Our Mr. Cartwright got stoned the night before the pageant and when he awoke to the glorious day he was aching. He took a couple of medicinal snorts and then a couple more. Slowly he managed to get into his Lafayette uniform, ingesting one cautious drink for each article of clothing, and when he was ready to drive to the battlefield, he concealed a flask of goblin juice on his person.

It was a most colorful and impressive spectacle, that pageant, and the presence of the two stately leaders, Washington and Lafayette, was inspiring to the populace. Midway of the proceedings, however, something seemed to go wrong with General Lafayette. He began, quite slowly, to tilt to one side. His tilt was in the direction of George Washington, who didn't appear to notice it. The tilt continued, and then suddenly turned into a fall, and the Marquis de Lafayette hit the sod, sprawling face upward, a look of alcoholic bewilderment on his handsome face.

He stared up at George Washington, who remained austere in the saddle, and meeting George's eye, he said:

"If I'd a-known that son of a bitch Lafayette got *this* drunk I never would have accepted the part."

■ ■

In the course of writing a recent novel about a cat, many of my friends stood by as technical advisers, for it would appear that everyone knows everything there is to be known about the life and times of the feline. Abel Green told me about a cat named Tommy Lamb. Tommy was the mascot and most important member of The Lambs, a Manhattan club for theatrical people, and was a cat of rather special attainments. He snoozed most of the time at one end of the club's bar, paying not the slightest heed to the tall talk of the drinking people. Whenever any person in the dining room ordered fish, this famous cat knew it instantly. *Not* when the fish was put on the fire. *Not* when the plate of fish was brought from the kitchen. Tommy knew that fish was being ordered the moment the diner spoke his wishes to the waiter— and the dining room was a fair distance away from the bar.

An actor said, perhaps, "I'll try the haddock." Tommy would come awake, get to his feet, and walk into the dining room and straight to the chair of the man who had ordered fish. He would sit by that chair until all the fish was gone, whether he got any or not. Abel Green said that many a skeptic, over the years, had refused to believe this, but that every one of them had been given a demonstration. Some had parted with large sums of money because they were firm in their skepticism.

Tommy Lamb is dead now. I understand his grandson is his successor at The Lambs, and that this grandson is a cat that can wear spectacles and read a newspaper and smoke a cigarette all at the same time. This doesn't interest me. I'm sorry I never got to see Tommy in action on the fish proposition. If he could really tell when a customer ordered fish, then I think Dr. Rhine and those other people down at Duke should have known about him. A new kind of extrasensory perception was taking place there in the club when Tommy was alive. Thought transference from man to cat. No, that's not right. From *fish* to cat. Or perhaps even from *fried fish* to cat. How the frontiers of knowledge continue to expand!

■　■

Such speculation leads me unerringly to the night in Nick's tavern on Greenwich Street when two gentlemen from the produce market were having some drinks at the bar and discussing ESP.

"Believe in it?" repeated the one named Corky. "My God I *have* it. I didn't know it was called extrasensible perception, but I've had it in me for years. In a special sorta way. I swear to you that I can look at a man, any man, and study him less than thirty seconds, and tell you whether he was a breast baby or a bottle baby."

"Horse shit," said the one named Fred. "Nobody could do that."

"I can do it," said Corky. "Wanna make a little bet?"

"How would we decide it?"

Corky glanced down the bar and saw several sportswriters at work with the glassware, and he chose one of their number, a man named Reilly.

"See that redhead down there?" he said. "I'll bet you ten bucks I can tell whether he was a breast baby or a bottle baby."

"And how'll you find it out?"

"I'll ask him." And so the bet was made and the two men walked down to the group of sportswriters and Corky approached the one called Reilly and first apologized for interrupting, and told about the bet, and asked if it was all right with Reilly, and Reilly said sure, go ahead. Corky looked him over carefully.

"You were a breast baby," he said.

"Wrong!" said Reilly. "Never had a tit in my mouth till I was nineteen years old!"

■　■

This happened, probably, at the same bar—for everything happened eventually at that bar. A guy walked in alone and ordered a drink. A few feet distant were a man and a woman, talking and drinking. All of a sudden the newcomer broke wind. Broke it beyond all repair. Broke it loudly. The other man glared at him, then took a step toward him and spoke in a tone of outrage: "What do you mean, farting before my wife!" The windbreaker replied: "Oh, I'm *so* sorry. I didn't know it was her turn."

■　■

In Hawaii the people who formerly lived on the Mainland and who now refer to themselves as *kamaainas* (old-timers) make an earnest effort to use fragments of the native tongue in their ordinary conversation. A girl is always a *wahine* and a white tourist is a *haole* (pronounced howly). To eat is *kaukau* (cowcow).

A man-about-Waikiki latched on to a beautiful little *haole* girl one afternoon and took her surfing and bought her a drink on the terrace at the Royal Hawaiian and then invited her to cocktails at his apartment.

At his digs (pad) he fed a couple of martinis into her, and put on some purring hi-fi, and took her onto his little terrace and showed her the sun going down over the Waianae range, and told her some magic tales of Hawaiian kings and Polynesian navigators. At last he said to her:

"Now would you like to *kaukau?*"

"Sure," said the girl. "Then maybe we could go get something to eat."

■   ■

Pardon me all to hell for talking shop again, but I've got to pass along one of my favorite newspaper stories. A vigorous and ambitious young man working for a wire service in Florida was covering a speedboat regatta in which the famous Gar Wood was taking part. In the midst of things there came a message from the wire service's regional headquarters in Atlanta, asking: "How old Gar Wood?" Our zestful boy reporter fired back: "Old Gar Wood fine, how you?"

■   ■

As a sanitary lead-in to the next story, let us consider the young mother in a town in the midwest where a prejudice existed against strong drink, and where children were supposed to be gently brainwashed on the subject.

This particular young mother did her propaganda work well, as she found out when her youngest son brought her a drawing he had made of a cowboy entering the swinging doors of a saloon.

"Don't worry, Mama," said the child. "He's not going in there to drink anything. He's just going in to shoot some men."

And so we proceed to . . .

■   ■

Frederick (formerly known as Sambo) and Edward (once called Mose) were two young men living in a small southern city and on a Saturday afternoon they took a walk into the downtown section to see what the white folks might be doing. After strolling around a while they sat down on the curb to rest. They were just across the street from Madame Polka Dot's fine house of ill repute.

A white man came out of the front door and down the steps and, pausing on the sidewalk, he went into a sort of conniption fit of shaking—much the same way a hen shakes after getting the business in a dusty farmyard.

Frederick and Edward made no comment.

In a little while another white man came out of Madame Polka

Dot's place and on the sidewalk launched himself into the same kind of seizure, exclaiming as he shook and shuddered, "Wow! Wow-eee!"

When a third white man went through this routine Frederick and Edward discussed the matter, and agreed that the merchandise in that house must be of superior quality. They agreed that they would never be able to buy any of it, but the spectacle of those white men in their after-ecstasy put temptation hard upon them. They decided that just one, Edward, should give it a try first. He stepped nervously to the front door and rang the bell and Madame Polka Dot answered and there was a brief conversation and into the house went Edward.

Frederick waited impatiently on the curb and nothing happened for six or eight minutes and then an upper window was opened and Edward poked his head out.

"Come awn in, Frederick!" he called out. "They don't mind goin' to bed wiv us—they jes' don't wanna go to *school* wiv us!"

■   ■

I first heard this story from an Englishman sitting on a terrace and looking out over the Aztec town of Tepoztlán in Mexico where skiis are seldom seen. I've heard it forty times since then. A young couple on their honeymoon checked in at a mountain lodge at a big ski resort, vanished into their suite, and were not seen again for three days. In the suite they themselves suddenly came to a realization that it would now be most embarrassing for them to appear downstairs before the other guests. The bridegroom applied his mind to the dilemma and came up with a solution. His sweet new wife would get into her ski togs and at dusk sneak out the back way of the hotel. Once outdoors she would cover herself with snow and pinch her cheeks to get them reddened up and then go bouncing in at the main entrance. The other people would think she had been out skiing all day.

And so they worked it, and she burst into the lodge, snowy

and pink and out of breath, and in a masterful burst of enthusiasm she cried out:

"Anyone who says screwin' isn't fun is a ski-ball!"

■　■

Heywood Broun, one of the great columnists, was a huge man and notorious for his slovenliness. He was once described as looking like an unmade bed, and again as a one-man slum.

Broun even managed to look sloppy wearing his uniform during World War I. It is said that General Pershing, during an inspection, paused before Heywood, looked at him carefully, and then asked:

"Did you fall down?"

■　■

The wedding was proceeding before the altar of St. Anne's-by-the-Waterfall and the cream of society was present. The ceremony reached the point where the ring was being placed on the bride's finger. A hush fell over the church. Then from one of the front pews came the high voice of a little girl:

"When does he sprinkle the pollen on her?"

■　■

Some years ago the New York Sanitation Department, indulging in one of those periodic but futile campaigns for a cleaner city, set up a special trash basket in Times Square and wired it for sound. A small transmitter-receiver was hidden in the can and a man with a mike was stationed in a window overlooking the scene.

The Associated Press reported that a woman came along and tossed a chewing-gum wrapper on the sidewalk. The trash can spoke sharply. "Madam," it said, "a cleaner New York is up to you."

The woman glared at the can but made no move to pick up the piece of paper.

"What is your name, madam?" the can now asked her.

"I don't speak to trash cans!" she snapped, and walked away.

■ ■

There was a fearsome time in the history of American journalism when many newspapers kept poets on their staffs. One such was Strickland Gillilan, who did ditties for a paper in Baltimore. The only poem of his that seems to have survived is, possibly, the finest poem ever written, and the shortest. It follows:

Lines on the Antiquity of Microbes
Adam
Had 'em.

Mr. Gillilan was in his office one day when another staff member stopped by to visit. After a while the visitor said he'd better get back to his desk and quit interfering with Mr. Gillilan's work.

"Don't go," said Mr. Gillilan. "The only thing I have to do all afternoon is let a poem."

■ ■

We were standing around under a glowering mountain peak on Ernest Munny's ranch just outside Alpine, Texas. Mr. Munny was telling about a long drought in a nearby county a few years back.

One of the local preachers had called a special evening session at his church, urging the whole community to attend and help him pray for rain. The day before the scheduled meeting the preacher ran into an old cowboy who had come in from one of the ranches.

"Chip," he said, "I wish you'd do me a big favor and come to the meeting tomorrow night and help us pray for rain."

Chip stroked his chin and squinted his eyes.

"Well, preacher," he said, "Ah'll come in, an' Ah'll pray, but Ah can tell you right now, it ain't gonna do no good long as this west wind keeps up."

■　■

The town of Fayetteville, Ark. (26,000 pop.) was once described by the architect Edward Durrell Stone, who was born there, as "a hotbed of tranquillity."

The town of Fayetteville, N. C. (51,000 pop.) stood in Sherman's path in 1865. When the Union army was within six miles of the town the mayor hastily called a meeting of the citizens. A few old men answered the summons, all other male citizens being off at war.

After the meeting was called to order old Mr. Horner raised himself to his feet with the aid of his cane and in a shrill voice spoke the following resolution:

"Mr. Mayor, we have no time to lose. I propose this: That we send to Mr. Hale's printing office and have him print ten thousand posters, to be distributed amid the Yankee army, telling them that they enter Fayetteville at the peril of their lives."

■　■

Makes me think of a story told me one day by Mr. Pete Ivey of North Carolina. In the course of a discussion on other matters Mr. Ivey brought up the name of a certain Colonel Tucker—a man whose exploits are said to have embodied the essential heroism of the Confederate fighting man.

This Colonel Tucker was skirmishing around one day, on sharpshooter duty, when he came upon a whole company of Yankee scum. The Union soldiers spread out in the woods the moment they caught sight of Colonel Tucker, and he quickly dropped behind a log and picked off three of the enemy. Then he crawled from tree to tree, getting a bead on one Yankee after another and dropping them in their tracks. At last one of the Yankees stuck his head out from behind a bush and yelled imploringly:

"My God, Colonel Tucker, you're not gonna shoot us *all?*"

■　■

I would remind Mr. Ivey that there was another great Southerner who fit the war. I have reference to Bill Arp, of Georgia. A reporter once asked Bill for the details of his career in the Confederate Army.

"Well," said Bill, "I reckon I'll have to give you the gory facts. I killed nearly as many Yankees as . . . well, as they did me."

■   ■

Peter Lind Hayes is, among many other things, an authority on the quips of the stuttering comic, Joe Frisco. One night Frisco appeared at a great benefit show which brought out many of the top stars of the entertainment world, including Enrico Caruso.

Frisco was standing in the wings beside Caruso and as the great tenor was being introduced, leaned over and whispered: "D-don't sing 'Darktown Strutters B-b-b-ball.' I u-u-u-u-use it f-f-for my f-f-finish."

■   ■

Wesley Stout passes along a story about Frankie Frisch, dating back to the era when Frisch was managing the old Gashouse Gang in St. Louis. Frisch was coaching at first base when Pepper Martin was called out on a close play by Umpire Bill Klem. Frisch gave forth a couple of jungle shrieks of protest and then fell over backwards in what looked to be a faint. His players began yelling "Heart attack! Heart attack!" and calling for cold water. But Umpire Klem was not to be intimidated. He pushed through the crowd of players, looked down at the fallen Frankie, and announced: "Frisch, dead or alive, you're outa the game!"

■   ■

It has come up Recitation Time again and by way of introduction, let me say that I know who wrote the following classic. A well-known author did it but it has been tampered with by others in recent years and I choose to present it to you tonight somewhat hopped up and slightly anonymous. Hold your hats!

RECITATION NO. 9

(The following paper was read by Biddeford Gimp, M.D., F.A.M., D.McL.B., before the Atlantic Medical Association in Convention Hall, Secaucus, New Jersey. Dr. Gimp is the author of *Gonads People Play* and *The History of Pelvic Burns*. He was Squibbs Professor of Thymus Disorders [sweetbread infarcts] at McGuff University until he took charge of the new out-patient department of the Hospital for the Distended.)

After twelve years of research in the Tannenbaum Laboratories at Muncie, Indiana, it is my privilege tonight to announce authoritatively that the war on post-alcoholic neuroticism, or uneasiness, has been won. In plain language, the so-called "hangover" has finally met its master and that long-sought panacea is coffee (Applause) administered as a hot enema. (Applause.)

As pointed out in 1907 by Doctors Holdfahrt and Grinn (see Fishbein's *A Flyswatter Is No Cure for Crabs*), caffeine has been used hypodermically for years to dispel the toxic coma superinduced by excessive drinking. That technique, however, is tedious, anathema to sensitive patients, dangerous to a degree, and can be employed properly only by a skilled practitioner. To quote Dr. Gerhardt Haulahss (*What Have Enzymes to Do With Impotence?*—Vol. VI., Page 606), the administration of caffeine (16cc., four and one-half per cent in aqua pura) is "a God damned infernal nuisance if there ain't a qualified doctor around."

The coffee enema, on the other hand, is readily available to all. It can be given in the home by any tyro, provided he does not try to play roulette with the patient's sphincters. The dosage is such as can be estimated or guessed at. Very strong coffee, as hot as can be tolerated without sending the patient leaping into the out-of-doors in improper dress, may be entertained, up to three quarts (or litres, if the patient is a society woman or British-born).

Only a few precautionary measures are necessary. A good

grade of coffee is recommended. Fastidious persons who insist on cream and sugar should be discouraged right away; an ideal way of doing this would be to advise them that it is unlikely that they will *taste* the injection. Also, those who demand that French coffee be employed should be cautioned against taking this mixture of chicory, concentrated lye and oxen's urine into the system at *either* end. It is widely known among the academics that there is not a sound bowel in any of the *arrondissements* of France. Indeed, the earlier Gallic obstetricians used French coffee in lieu of ergot during parturition. (Applause. Cries of "Hear! Hear!") Many patients, facing up to this treatment, will weep pitifully, and plead with the doctor to use Irish coffee; be firm with them. As for Italian *espresso,* it is quite suitable although the patient should be strapped down and dosed liberally with scopolamine before he is rammed.

Of seven thousand cases observed at the Tannenbaum clinic only seven failed to respond to the coffee enema treatment for drunken aftermath. It may be worth noting that out of those seven, four were dead on arrival. The following cross-section may be of interest to the members:

Case 542. Mrs. M., 52-years-old, blue eyes and suffering from hyperacidity. Was resonant on percussion. When brought in seemed to be in a state of *talkative* rigor mortis. Respiration wheezy, rales in right lung and quantities of gin and rose water in trachea and the bronchi. After three quarts of coffee were spilled by nurse, who mistook the target for the Carlsbad Caverns, another dosage (blend of Old Dutch and Yuban drip) was managed effectively. Mrs. M. soon rose screaming from the enema-table, started to bid in an imaginary bridge game, seized her girdle and began swinging it around her head and then went tripping gaily into the night.

Case 234. Adolph Z., machinist's helper, 36-years-old, has common-law wife and is fond of sweets. Secret drinker. Has boss-persecution complex and Hutchinson's teeth. Found in gutter near fashionable night club. Both hands caught in his own fly. Claimed he was wrestling with an anaconda. Subdued by Patrolmen Shadley and Grommet and held on ground while coffee (Maxwell House Electra-perk) was siphoned in until his colon was distended from sigmoid to cecum. Howled like a castrated mink for two minutes, contending law officers should have "blown on it first." Then got up calmly and began to tinker with engine of police car, mumbling that it was a Baldwin locomotive about to give birth. Complete cure.

Case 104. Armand F., apprentice procurer, and organist at St. Ziphany's Church in Glendale, California. Found trapped in organ bellows which, in his delirium, he imagined to be his mother. On being rescued, railed at intern who was administering coffee per rectum (two quarts Medaglia D'Oro black). Maintained loudly that someone was singing off-key. At clinic was given two more minutes of the stop-and-go process, by which the same coffee is injected in little spurts, during which he giggled and gasped; then got to his feet, began to sway his hips, and asked the head nurse if she had any ashes she would like to have hauled. Gratifying cure.

Case 320. Marigold P., 14-years-old, body three years older. Had serious uncle-father-brother urges, plus strong tendencies toward cousins. Analysts unable to interpret her dreams. Drinks only on Thursday nights when she retires to closet and plays naughty, alone. Juvenile formula No. 3 (two parts Pride of Columbia regular, to one part circus lemonade) used with amazing success. Patient felt so exhilarated she vanished before treatment completed. Last seen running into Porter's Woods hand-in-hand with Dr. Pesorie, a teadrinker.

Case 304. Emanuel O., 41-years-old, a casting director for musical shows. Fell off an actress while drunk, fracturing pelvis and little finger. Eight quarts of coffee (Chase & Sanborn) were swirled into him, one by one, but failed to bring relief. When six drops of Coty's No. 3 perfume were added to the ninth quart, response was instantaneous. Ran from clinic naked and appearing to feel no pain from broken bones. Was heard crying "Sylvia! Laura! Mandy!" as he vanished into the gloaming.

Case 51. Rev. Turk S., 73-years-old, pastor of small church in Norwalk Corners. While drinking for medicinal purposes (to ease his asthma) found himself committing a carnal sin with an innkeeper's niece. Overcome by shame, his pants still unbuttoned, he arrived at clinic shouting, "For Christ's sake, give it to me!" While we were giving it to him (Martinson Red mixed with Savarin) he glanced down and saw something that made him believe he was The Devil, wearing a long red tail. Prayers were spoken and an extra dosage prepared, a demitasse with a teaspoon of Aunt Jemima Buckwheat Flour stirred in. While this was being administered he kept pleading with the attendants, "Oh, that's good! Try it on the front! Try it on the front!" This quick response was edifying to all concerned. Patient returned to his church and continued his work. He has recently written the clinic that his asthma has cleared up but that he often grows quite flatulent in the pulpit.

Case 6,502. Wilbur D., 92-years-old, cabinet officer under three presidents, militiaman, student of Parsee literature, drunk since the False Armistice. When first treated (one gallon Chock Full O' Nuts) had long period of delusions, thought he was the man playing the flute in the 1776 painting. Begged the doctors to cut him down from the museum wall, crying, "Do something constructive, you communists, instead of shoving all that machinery into my butt!" Following treatment there was a sign of improvement, for he now believed himself to be only a *copy* of the man in the original picture, and the *drummer* instead of the flute player. Arrested case.

In conclusion, gentlemen, let me say that we at Tannenbaum are most happy over the way this project has worked out. We now move into other fields. Inspired by our success with the coffee enema, we are approaching other problems by the same direction. At present we believe we are about to cure the common cold. All I can tell you about the experiment is this: the cure, if it works, will be effected by what we call a *hard* enema —large pills containing tannic acid, licorice, a slight amount of the Buckwheat Flour, and two new drugs found near Roswell in New Mexico. These pills are about the size of ping pong balls and are shot into the patient with a rivet gun. It is my hope to report favorably on this experiment at our next . . . uh . . . kaffeeklatsch. (Laughter. Applause.)

BUSKIN' AT A
CENTRAL PARK POON-IN

In my latter years I have developed a bum liver, from drinking, with the consequence that I have been looking upon many aspects of progressive civilization with a jaundiced eye. Dancing, for example. No . . . come to think of it I was making critical remarks about dancing back before World War II. I said that it was a foolish pursuit and that no good would ever come of it. Just *look* what's come of it. Whippin'—that's what they need.

I don't often find myself siding with the Shah of Persia, but I value his opinion in this area of human frivolity. George R. Stewart has a story in one of his books about a visit the Shah paid to Paris, many years ago. He was taken to a society ball where he observed the rich folks of Paris leaping and swirling around the room in a Viennese pigeonwing and, mindful of his own dancing girls back home, he asked: "Can't these people *hire* someone to do this for them?"

There is merit, too, in the opinion of Maxwell Bodenheim who wrote back in his Chicago days that since the dawn of history dancing had been one of the more adroit female ruses for the sexual stimulation of the male. "A young woman," he continued, "who embraces a man while he is being assailed by primitive drum beats and bacchanalian horn tootings, may pretend that she is interested only in the technique of dancing. I wonder if the same young woman, naked in bed with a man, would insist that she is only testing out the mattress."

There is still another approach to the question. I used to be well acquainted with a gentleman who has been a fixture in broadcasting for many years, a public idol of sorts, admired and even worshiped by hordes of American housewives. Once we were off on a trip together, helling it up in a big resort hotel, and he asked me why I wasn't dancing. I said I thought it was silly.

"Well," he grinned, "I suppose I do too, but it's the quickest way I know of finding out if you can bang a gal."

■ ■

Rummaging through the vast welter of notes I have accumulated during my adult years, I found the other day a few lines which may be of historical importance; it was a report on a minor incident in San Francisco in the year 1943. It might be the very beginning of the New Era among our young people, the rise of the Beats and Hippies and Teeny-boppers.

On that day in 1943 a police inspector spotted a man walking steadily backward along the sidewalk on busy Powell Street. The inspector approached the man and asked him why.

"I like," said the unnamed man, "to study the expressions on the faces of the people who are walking behind me."

He was wearing a beard.

■ ■

Which brings up Dick Bradford. When the beard thing first hit the enlightened few, Dick decided to go along with the trend and started cultivating chin whiskers. The hair came out looking rather ragged and uneven. Dick's friends began making remarks. One said: "You're beginning to look like an armpit." He stayed with it, for he was brought up in the French Quarter of New Orleans. Then a day came when he felt that his beard was starting to shape up into an aesthetic triumph. He approached another friend, a man whose artistic opinion he respected, and asked for an evaluation.

"Looks like the formal gardens at the House of Usher," said the friend. Dick shaved.

■   ■

I could never send in My Most Embarrassing Moment to the newspapers. There are just too many of them to choose from, and I would have to classify my examples under the heading, "My Most Embarrassing Moment . . . of This Week."

Here is one that's fresh in my mind—a thing that's supposed to happen only in books. Normally I get my haircut in a small town in the New York suburbs, but sometimes I like to have the job done by a barber on 55th Street in Manhattan. Just last week I was waiting my turn in this city barber shop. My guy had a little kid in the chair and the little kid's mother was present, a handsome young woman who could have passed for a sex wagon. Had on stretch pants. When the kid's haircut was finished, she did a lot of flouncing around the shop getting him bundled up, and her figure was volatile and rubbery and altogether splendid. As they say in novels, my loins ached. So she took her departure and I got in the chair and said: "That woman with the kid sure has a high ass. Highest-assed woman I believe I've ever seen." Said my barber, spacing his words and speaking in a stern tone: "That high-assed woman happens to be my wife."

■   ■

Nipsey Russell, the Negro comic, says that at 3 o'clock one morning he was standing at the corner of 34th Street and Broadway in New York, waiting for a crosstown bus.

He waited and he waited and he waited. Still no bus, so he waited some more. Across the street he saw a party of seven or eight white men and women come out of a tavern. They walked a few yards to the corner, opposite where Nipsey was standing, and they stopped there for a bit more conversation before going their separate ways. Nipsey glanced impatiently up 34th Street once again, and no bus was in sight, so now he called out to the people across the way, "Hey!"

141

They swung around to face in his direction and then he hollered a question:

"Crosstown . . . bus . . . run . . . all . . . night . . . long?"
In one fine chorus the white people sang out:
"Doo-dah! Doo-dah!"

■   ■

You've got to hand it to European Man. He's just a bit smarter than we are. For centuries it was the custom in many rural parts of Europe for the man to always walk ten paces in front of his wife. This custom was at last changed. After World War II it became the practice for the woman to walk ten paces ahead. The reason: the great number of land mines left unexploded all over the continent.

■   ■

The teacher was putting on a little demonstration to illustrate for her second-graders how tricky the sense of taste can become. She summoned little Richard to the front of the room and put a blindfold on him and told him she was going to have him taste several things and see if he could tell what they were. In each instance she would give him a spoken clue.

She gave him a small nibble of bread and said it often came with butter and he got it. She gave him a bite of pickle and said it was once a cucumber and he missed. Next she fed him a bit of apple pie on a spoon and told him it was something special his mother did. He tasted it and tasted it and couldn't seem to get the answer, and because he had been such a willing performer, the teacher gave him a second clue.

"What is it," she said, "that your daddy says he wants at night when he comes home from work?"

Richard tasted again, still perplexed, and from the back of the room came a warning cry:

"Don't swaller it, Dickie! It's a piece of a tail!"

■　■

　　One day Ed Sheehan, broadcaster, bon vivant and part-time beachcomber, telephoned me at the Royal Hawaiian Hotel and said he hated like all hell to do it but he had a big favor to ask of me.

　　"I know how it is," he said, "with you professional writers—how people are always wanting you to read their manuscripts. But I think we are now good enough friends that you won't mind glancing through this thing of mine. Frankly, I've been trying for ten years to write *the* novel about Hawaii. I can get just so far in the story and then I bog down. I have the manuscript of the beginning of the book, and I feel certain you could go over it and suggest a way for me to proceed."

　　I groaned inwardly. This is one of the truly godawful penalties of being a published writer. But Ed Sheehan had gone out of his way to be helpful to me, and so I said for him to send it over, and then I began worrying about what I should tell him in case the stuff turned out to be impossible, which was almost a sure thing.

　　Then the package came and inside was a single sheet containing the complete manuscript, as follows:

　　This poor little whore was sitting on the beach in the rain and it was a terrible sight.
　　Then

That's as far as Sheehan had been able to get on The Great Hawaiian Novel.

■　■

　　On the other hand, when Jim Moran sent me *his* manuscript, it turned out to be much longer. It, too, appeared to be the beginning of a novel—a book with a screeching potential, judging from Jim's sample, which went this way:

One of my good friends, a masochistic, beatnik, Christian

143

do-gooder, is employed as slop-jar washer in the biggest whorehouse on Lanoni Island, the well-known jungle leper colony.

He continued bugging me for a couple of years to come down and visit him but I kept putting him off.

Then I got involved in divorce proceedings and had to spend considerable time with lawyers, process-servers, detectives, false witnesses, courtroom officials, judges, and others in this field.

When it was finally over I felt rather soiled and urgently in need of a more wholesome atmosphere. Just then another cable arrived from my friend on Lanoni offering me a job as his assistant. I accepted with alacrity.

It is my understanding that Jim went ahead and finished his book and got it published. I'm eager to get my hands on it. I want to know how it comes out.

■　　■

The aforementioned Ed Sheehan wrote me once that years ago a streetcar conductor in his home town in Massachusetts peed the name of a local schoolteacher in the snow and ruined her for life.

I passed this sociological anecdote along to Dick Bradford in Santa Fe and Dick sent me a variation of the tale. Dick's snow-job had a Vermont setting.

The mother of a teen-age girl in this Vermont town went over to the home of a neighbor and in great indignation said to the lady of the house, "I just want you to come out here and see something!" They went out into the winter landscape and the mother of the young girl pointed to a snowbank where somebody had peed the name of her daughter Dorothy.

The mother of Dorothy now demanded of her neighbor: "I want you to punish your boy for doing such a disgraceful thing as this."

The boy's mother looked again at the peed word, and said,

"Why, my son couldn't have done that. That's your daughter's own handwriting."

■   ■

A spate of toothbrush jokes went into circulation in the middle 1960s, all concerned with the violation of hygienic principles. My toothbrush story dates back fifty years when the Speaker of the House of Representatives was a rough-hewn political rascal out of the Midwest. At the national convention of his party he and another member of Congress shared a hotel room and one morning the other statesman emerged from the bathroom and spoke accusingly to the Speaker.

"Did you," he demanded, "use *my* toothbrush?"

The Speaker stared at him a moment in hesitation, then spoke.

"My God," he said, "was that yourn? I thought it was one somebody left here."

■   ■

A Southern Illinois mule wandered near the grounds of a traveling circus one morning and came upon a zebra, idly cropping away at some dry grass underneath a tree.

"Hey, sport," the mule called out. The zebra lifted her head and contemplated the stout peasant with interest.

"Whadda ya do around here for kicks?" went on the mule.

"Oh," said the zebra, "we do about what everyone else does."

"In that case," said the mule, "git them crazy pajamas off and less git at it!"

■   ■

A gentleman visiting in Maine encountered a small boy and in the course of their conversation, asked him if he could read.

"Kinda," said the boy.

"What do you mean, kinda?"

"When I get to the crossroad," the boy explained, "I can tell how far but I can't tell where to."

■　　■

Roy Rogers was born Leonard Slye on a pig farm near Duck
Run, Ohio. When he had reached the height of his fame as
Hollywood's most glamorous cowboy star, he happened to be
making a personal appearance in Chicago, and he got the idea
for a little experiment.

It was a studio requirement that Roy always wear his cowboy
duds in public and one day he had been out walking in the Loop,
attired in his sky-blue outfit and big white hat. Crowds of people
pushed him around, wanting his autograph, wanting to talk to
him, to touch him. It was that way every time he went out.

Back in his hotel he thought about how nice it would be for a
change to walk the city streets without being recognized. It had
been a dozen years since he had worn a business suit, but now
he called in a tailor and ordered one, a plain blue serge, and a
pair of black oxfords, and a white shirt and plain necktie and an
ordinary hat. He put all these things on and went for another
walk. Nobody gave him a second look. He enjoyed the sensation
so much that the next day when he boarded "The Chief" for
Los Angeles, he was still wearing the civvies. He lounged in the
club car and no one recognized him and then, walking through
the moving train he arrived in a vestibule between cars and came
face to face with a man walking in the opposite direction. The
two stared at each other and Roy recognized a former resident
of Duck Run, Ohio. But before he could say a word the other
man cried out:

"Great God A'Mighty! Leonard Slye! *Whirr you been?*"

■　　■

A drummer arrived in a small Ozark town and was directed to Miz Mudge's boardin' house. When he arrived there,
Miz Mudge's husband was sitting on the front porch, resting.

"I'm in sort of a hurry," said the drummer, "where's the place?"

Mr. Mudge waved around toward the back of the house, and
the visitor hurried out to the vine-covered privy.

146

When he came back Mr. Mudge asked if everything had been all right.

"Yes," said the drummer, "but the flies are pretty fierce out there."

"I know," said Mr. Mudge. "You should have waited till the dinner hour, when they're all in the dinin' room."

■   ■

The celebrated Belgian author Maurice Maeterlinck was hired once by Samuel Goldwyn and transported to Hollywood for the purpose of writing a screenplay. Salary: $10,000 a week. He told Mr. Goldwyn that he didn't quite know how to go about writing a film, and the producer advised him to go home, take one of his best books, and adapt it as a movie. After two or three weeks Maeterlinck's script was delivered and handed to Mr. Goldwyn. A short time later he came storming out of his office, waving the scenario angrily, and shouting, "My God, the hero is a *bee!*"

■   ■

L. Gower Felk, a retired stockbroker, lived in comfort on his small Westchester estate with a gorilla named Pam for a pet. Mr. L. Gower Felk was fond of his gorilla. Deeply.

There came a time when Pam began to exhibit signs of illness. She lost interest in food, didn't want to play games with her master, just sat around and moped. Mr. Felk called in a vet and the vet recognized that something was wrong, and said he'd take Pam away and keep her under observation for a while and make some tests.

In a few days he was back with Pam. The trouble, he said, was simple. She needed the attention of a male gorilla. Mother nature was demanding that she be bred. If she was not mated, and soon, she would just pine away and maybe die.

A shocking idea, that, to Mr. Felk. What should he do?

"You've got to find a male gorilla to mate her with," said the vet.

"And how do I go about that?"

"Well," said the vet, "you have problems. No circus would let you use any male gorilla they might have. Zoos wouldn't consider the proposition. You've got to find someone like yourself who has a gorilla for a pet, but a male gorilla, and then you've got to talk that person into letting the two mate. You've still got problems. There are not many individuals who keep gorillas around for pets, but I can put you in touch with a man in France who might know of someone."

In time Mr. Felk learned that there was a gentleman farmer in Bavaria who had a male gorilla in his household, and a correspondence began.

The Bavarian man balked at first, but Mr. Felk was persuasive and after a while the Bavarian said he might be willing for his male gorilla to come to America and do the job, "but never alone." He pointed out that he was just as fond of *his* gorilla as Mr. Felk was of Pam, and he would not permit his pet to travel unless he came along. If he and his gorilla undertook the trip, they would not want to just go bang-bang and then turn around and head home—they'd like to spend a couple of weeks looking at New York. The whole project, then, would add up to about ten thousand dollars. If Mr. Felk was willing to pay that sum, the Bavarian would agree.

Mr. Felk was outraged. Ten thousand dollars! To get a gorilla . . . to get a gorilla . . . No, by God, he'd never submit to such bald robbery! Yet he still had the problem of the sulking Pam, and he sat down and thought for a long time, and then he summoned his gardener, a large Pole named Sigismund.

"Sigismund," said Mr. Felk, "you have worked for me all these years and we have become good friends, and I have treated you well and you have treated me well. Now I have a great favor to ask. I know that you like Pam almost as much as I do. You have seen how she has been behaving lately. She is sick, Sigismund."

He told the gardener the whole story, and the big Pole was all but weeping when the telling thrust came.

"Sigismund," said Mr. Felk, "I will give you twenty-five hundred dollars if you will take care of this Pam matter for me."

"Oh no!" cried Sigismund. "Never! You have been good boss, I like work for you, but not this! I not do! Never!"

But Mr. Felk kept talking, and finally jumped his offer to five thousand, and told Sigismund he could take the money and go to Miami Beach and stay a month, two months, and live in the grandest hotel there, and lie around on the beach where there were hundreds of beautiful young girls wearing those skimpy little bikini things, eager to leap into bed with such a big strong fellow as Sigismund, and after that he'd still have enough money to go over to Bermuda, where the bikinis were even skimpier and the girls more beautiful and eager, and by now Sigismund's eyes had widened and he was breathing rather hard, and finally he exclaimed:

"Mr. Felk, I'll do it. But I got three conditions."

"Name them."

"First," said Sigismund, "nobody is to ever know about this, nobody except you and me. Hokay?"

"Quite reasonable. Okay."

"Second, I don't have to kiss her."

Mr. Felk smiled. "That seems an altogether reasonable request. Condition agreed to. And what's the third, Sigismund?"

"The children have gotta be raised Catholic."

■   ■

It is recorded that the actress Shelley Winters, on being told that she had buck teeth, delivered herself of a nice line: "I've seen some that are bucker."

Back yonder in the midlands we had a saying: "His teeth were so bucked he could bite the heart out of a watermelon through a picket fence." When I took up residence on the Atlantic Seaboard, I found that the eastern style was: "He could eat a tomato through a tennis racquet."

Another little story that had a good run in the Midwest concerned the farm boy and the first banana he ever saw. His paw brought half a dozen of them home from town and handed one to the boy.

"Clem," he said, "that there's a bannaner. Go take it out in the yard and eat it."

Later when Clem returned his paw asked him how he liked the bannaner.

"Oh," said Clem, "it was middlin' good, but it's shore got a lotta cob to it."

■   ■

Footnote to the History of Music in America: Ulysses S. Grant was once asked to state his preferences in music. His reply: "I know only two tunes. One of them is 'Yankee Doodle' and the other isn't."

■   ■

Whenever I have talked about or written about Sidney B. Whipple, people have assumed that he was a fictional character, a myth. My God, I used to have a good friend named Henry F. Misselwitz! I introduced Henry to another man at a cocktail party in the Waldorf-Astoria one day.

As they shook hands, the man said, "What was that name again?"

"Misselwitz," said Henry. The man regarded him for a bit with deep interest.

"Look," he said, "it must be all this damn racket, but would you mind giving it to me again?"

Henry was fairly accustomed to this sort of thing, but he didn't cotton to this particular guy.

"*Missel—witz!*" he said.

The man grinned. "Oh," he said. "I got it now. You know, for a minute there I'd have sworn you said 'Misselwitz.'"

Sidney B. Whipple was no myth. In many respects he was the greatest man I have ever known. I could fill this book with a recitation of his talents. One of these was his ability to tell Cockney stories, a knack he picked up during a newspaper tour of duty in London. Most of Sid's stories were ribald and Rabelaisian or both, but somehow they never seemed so under his deft telling. This one, for example:

Walking along a street in London a little old lady heard a blast of language coming out of a manhole. It was improper language, violent and profane. It upset her. She walked over to the manhole and peered into it and called out: "My good man! What is happening down there?"

In a moment a head, of sorts, came slowly out of the hole. It was the head of a man, wearing a greasy old cap, unshaven, his nose bulbous and empurpled, his eyes bleary.

"What *is* the matter?" the old lady repeated.

"I'll tell ya, lydy," said the grimy one. "We're stock-tykin' today and we're two tunna shid short."

■   ■

And one more from Sidney, concerning the same unclean character of the London sewers. With several of his associates he had been working underneath a seminary attended by young girls. It came on noontime and these gentlemen got their lunch pails and sat themselves on whatever ledges or projections that were available. Our old friend of the bulbous nose took a long glance at his immediate surroundings before opening his pail, and growled: "Cor blimey, what a spawt! All piss 'n' curl-papers an' not a solid lump to stick yer candle in whilst ya eat yer lunch!"

RECITATION NO. 10

Let me tell you (said Ed Sheehan of Honolulu) the story of a great unsung hero. It is a story of World War II and it involves a near-miracle. In my opinion it ranks with the great cloak-and-dagger thrillers of world literature.

It is about a young Navy guy, an enlisted man; unhappily I cannot tell you his name. If I can ever find his name I am going to lead a campaign for a towering monument commemorating his achievement.

This young man . . . but first let me tell you how things were in Honolulu right after the Jap raid. This city was black dark every night and the curfew was rigidly enforced. Heavy fines were imposed on anyone who allowed so much as a sliver of light to show, or who was caught smoking a cigarette outdoors.

So this young sailor made it with a dame out in Kahala. He was a fellow maybe nineteen, well set up, and he picked up this married dame in Waikiki and they went out to her house where she had plenty of whisky and some nice records. The gal was doing her patriotic duty, and the windows were blacked out, and there was a small blue light near the phonograph which was purring away with some Glen Miller, and they were all settled down in glorious concordance, when suddenly another purring, an *alien* purring, was heard—her husband's automobile pulling into the driveway.

Our hero wasted not a fraction of a second, for he knew the husband to be a ship's officer of enormous ferocity, fiercer than Victor McLaglen with a load on. Out the back door went our boy wearing not a stitch of clothes. Into the tropic night he scrambled on all fours, like an ape in the forest primeval. He dodged in and out of the shrubbery and coconut trees, for he was expecting gunfire to break out at any instant. He was shaking like a whore in the confessional, and trying to take stock of his situation. Here he was, crouched and skulking in the swankiest part of Honolulu, naked as a jaybird, ten long miles from his ship, with the most thickly populated area of the Hawaiian Islands lying between him and sanctuary.

Somehow he located his borrowed car which he had parked half a block from the house. He quickly got into the driver's seat and crouched there, shivering for a moment. There was nothing to do but take the chance. It was approximately the same chance that the celebrated snowball was supposed to have in the equally celebrated Hell.

And so this little guy somehow managed to drive all the way

through Waikiki, through downtown Honolulu, out the Nimitz Highway, and through the main gate of Pearl Harbor, at a time of history and a time of night when Honolulu was the most jittery city in the entire world—crawling with cops, shore patrol, military police, secret service, foreign spies, and God knows what else—and every single member of that vast and shadowy crowd suffering from triggeritis—and here was our boy, driving straight through the center of it all *without a stitch of clothes on.* How he ever made it remains one of the truly great mysteries of World War II. It was impossible . . . and yet that boy did it. It almost had to be concatenation of many miracles that would permit him to chug his way past hundreds of cops and patrols and sentries and air wardens and even the marines at the Pearl Harbor gates without once being challenged.

I have been told that the boy reached his ship and stumbled aboard, still naked, and mumbled to the officer of the deck, "Crap game," and then collapsed. A great American hero, beyond any doubt.

JOKES THAT
GENERALLY GO WELL
IN LIMA, PERU

As the author of a 32-inch shelf of bright and lively books, and of bright and lively magazine pieces beyond counting, I get a lot of bright and lively mail. I also get a lot of mail of such deadly dreariness that it would put a fence post to sleep. Many of my correspondents send stories and the majority of these are lacking in quality, but now and then a tale comes in that makes it all worth while.

I used to get letters from an official of a state penitentiary out West, great sprawling missives running sometimes to twenty pages and dealing usually with the depravities to be encountered inside prison walls. If it is of interest to you, the depravities to be encountered inside prison walls are the same as the depravities to be encountered outside prison walls. In one of his letters this man told me the huckleberry story. It is a sad story, and touches the heart.

In a Western mountain town, during the Depression of the 1930s, there lived a man named Gowan, proprietor of a small hardware store. He was known far and wide for his sweet disposition, his unfailing good nature and he seemed to have the world by the tail until . . . disaster struck him blow after blow after blow, all within a single month. His troubles began with pressure from the wholesalers and suddenly he found himself without his store. He scouted around but there would have been no job for Francis of Assisi in those desperate times. At last he wandered homeward, only to find a note from his wife telling him that she had run off with a neighbor gentleman who was one of Gowan's best friends. Shortly after that his automobile was repossessed, and then the mortgage on his house was foreclosed.

He had to do something. He didn't have enough money to buy food. He thought of the mountains back of the town and remembered that their slopes were covered with huckleberry bushes and that this was the season. He borrowed two tin buckets and went trudging up the mountain and worked half a day, and then came back down with his buckets full of berries.

Now he started going from house to house, trying to sell his huckleberries, but nobody seemed to want them. Gowan was a man of backbone, however, and he stuck with it. At length he arrived at a neat cottage and knocked on the door and a rather handsome lady responded. She told him she never bartered with salesmen on her front porch and that he should go to the rear door.

As he was trudging around the house, carrying his two buckets of berries, she was busily shucking off her clothes while she made her way to the back door. He was standing there, and had put his buckets down, when she opened the door. She was naked.

"Come on in," she smiled, "and we'll talk about those berries."

He stood and looked at her a long while, and then his face began to crease up and he swallowed hard a couple of times and then he burst into tears.

"Well!" exclaimed the naked lady. "What in the name of God's the matter with *you?*"

He stood for a moment, fighting back his sobs, and then he wiped the tears from his face, and he said:

"The whole world has turned against me. I lose my nice little store that it took me fifteen years to build up. My wife runs away with my best friend. They come and take my car away from me. Then they foreclose the mortgage on my house. I can't get a job anywhere in this town and now . . ." he sobbed a couple of times, ". . . and now *you* wanna fuck me out of my huckleberries!"

■ ■

I doubt that anyone here has ever heard of Benny Cleveland, but to me he occupies a special niche in American history. He figures in a book about Nantucket history, written a dozen years ago by Frank B. Gilbreth, Jr.

Benny Cleveland was a jack-of-all-trades on the island of Nantucket, specializing in doing odd jobs for women whose husbands were away at sea. Frank Gilbreth describes him as "a rather vague citizen, and so innocent and harmless that no scandal could ever attach itself to him." As a result of this reputation, when Nantucket women were ill or expecting babies and their husbands were away, they would hire Benny to sleep at night in their houses. Benny enjoyed this type of work, and wanted to get more of it, so he ran an ad in the paper, saying:

"Women slept with, twenty-five cents a night. Nervous women, fifteen cents extra."

■ ■

Here is an item of a common genus, a takeoff on inter-office communiqués. The people who get the most fun out of such parodies are usually the people who compose the original monstrosities, and who never cease composing them in the time-honored and flatulent manner.

CONFIDENTIAL MEMO TO CLASS "A" EXECUTIVES

The Systems and Procedure Division of the Corporation will activate its RAPE Program in all departments by mid-summer. Our target date is July 15th. RAPE is the designation for the phaseout of many departments of the Company (Retire Aging Personnel Early) and applies to executives below the "B" Class.

Employees who are RAPED will have an opportunity to seek employment in other departments. Those who decline to seek such employment may request a review of their records before discharge. This phase of the cut-back shall be known in future communications as SCREW (Survey of Capabilities of Retired Early Workers).

In line with the Corporation's paternalistic and benevolent policy, there will be no cold and abrupt cut-off; each affected employee will be afforded a final chance after he has been both RAPED and SCREWED. This last chance is BUGRD (Board of Upper Gradient Retroactive Departures). Every affected worker will be BUGRD if he shows the slightest inclination to accept it.

Let it be understood that employees who are RAPED may be permitted just one SCREWING. The way is clear for them to be BUGRD, however, as many times as they wish.

With all good wishes,
The Management.

■   ■

There are more hazards to the business of driving an automobile than there are cars burdened with factory defects, women drivers, men drivers, homosexual drivers and bees that fly in through the windows.

I was driving along Bedford Road, exercising care, and the car radio was going. A New York disk jockey was interviewing a girl fresh up from Puerto Rico with her guitar. She was eager to get work in the Manhattan night clubs.

Disk jockey: "Tell me, Maria, what type of songs do you like to do best?"

Maria: "I like best fulk songs."

My car swerved sharply, went onto the shoulder of the road, and I came within half a foot of hitting a tree. When I recovered my equilibrium I heard myself murmur: "Don't they all?"

■   ■

Chuck Daggett, a warm friend in my Hollywood days, came out of the Missouri Ozarks and was quite handy at telling stories of that region. His grandfather was one of his best characters. Grandpa Daggett went through World War I convinced that he was surrounded by German spies. One day he summoned his grandson, peered around a few corners to make sure no alien snoops were eavesdropping, and then said:

"Chuck, they's a new German spy in town. He's got a hull trunkload of pencils, so if anybody offers you a pencil don't take it. These here are German spy pencils. You know how ever'body takes a pencil when they get ready to write something, and first off they lick the point with their tongue so's it will write good and black. Well, this here German spy hands you a pencil and says for you to write something. So you stick the point in yore mouth and lick it and . . . *it blows the whole toppa yore head off!*"

■   ■

It was General Iron Pants Johnson who spoke in a mildly critical manner of another government personality in Washington, calling the man a revolving son of a bitch. Asked to define the term, General Johnson said: "It means that he's a son of a bitch any way you look at him." Under this definition I consider myself to be a revolving pessimist, and I have long been interested in further definitions aimed at distinguishing between pessimists and optimists. My favorite, I think, is this: An optimist is a man who believes that this is the best of all possible worlds; a pessimist is a man who fears that it is.

A female relative of mine has sent me a little story touching on this point. There were twin boys named Charlie and John, seven years old. Charlie was a haggard pessimist and John a devout optimist. At Christmastime their parents gave Charlie a new bike, a set of electric trains and a pair of skiis. Santa brought for John a single gift—a plastic bag full of horse manure.

When Grandma arrived in the living room Christmas morning she wanted to know the nature of the loot each boy got. Charlie the Pessimist spoke: "I got a bike but the steering wheel won't work, and a set of trains that won't stay on the tracks, and a pair of skiis but they keep falling off me." Little John the Optimist was sitting on the floor, his hand in the bag of manure. He was feeling around as if searching for something.

"I think," he said, "that Santa Claus brought me a pony, but I haven't been able to find it yet."

■　■

This high school girl came up to New York from some town in Georgia, probably Valdosta, and got herself a job running an elevator down around Fourteenth Street. She didn't know a soul at first, and was ignorant of Big City ways, and then one day she met another girl on the bus and they became acquainted. The other girl, whose name was Marigold, had been in New York a long time and so she asked the Georgia girl how she was making out.

"Okay," said the Valdosta girl, "but here it is only November and I get mighty cold. Freeze my laigs off, nilly."

Marigold glanced at her new friend's legs. "Well, no wonder," she said. "You can't go around barelegged like that in New York. Tell you what you do. Buy yourself some of them things they call leoturds. They're like stockin's go clear up to your waist. They'll keep you warm."

They didn't see each other again for about a week, then Marigold spotted Valdosta on the bus again. They sat together riding downtown and Marigold asked her friend how she was doing, and Valdosta said fine, and then Marigold asked if she had got them leoturds, and Valdosta flipped out her legs to show that she had.

"How you like them?" asked Marigold.

"Fine," said Valdosta, "except ever' time I fot it blows my sneakers off."

■　■

Doug Gilbert was one of the most colorful newspapermen I ever had the privilege of working with in New York City. Doug was in turn a general reporter, a rewrite man, a movie critic and then he became drama critic for the old *World-Telegram.* He was competent at all of these jobs and quite a stylist in his writing. He did a splendid book on the history of American vaudeville, and another on the nation's popular songs.

Doug was an irascible man. He held grudges proudly, and had a plenty of them. His life was one minor tragedy right after another, and he bellowed his indignations into the blue. He committed blunders of classical stature day after day, but he himself was never at fault—vague outside influences were at work on him. Nature was against him.

His ambition was to get out of the newspaper business and take his proper place in Broadway theatrical production, and I remember when the big break came. A man important in the theatrical world called him and indicated that he was thinking of giving Doug an important job in his production company. He would start at twice the salary he was getting on the paper. They arranged to meet in a booth at a quiet restaurant just off Times Square.

This was Doug's great opportunity—the thing he had dreamed about. He sat in the booth opposite the producer. They had a couple of drinks and then they ordered dinner. Doug got a plate of clam spaghetti. They talked along as they ate and things were going swimmingly. Then something happened. Doug had his mouth full of clam spaghetti. Before he could catch himself, before he could even turn his head, a tremendous paroxysm seized him, his mouth flew open, and he sneezed a mighty sneeze, splattering that Broadway producer from chest to scalp with clam spaghetti.

The Savior himself wouldn't have hired Doug after that.

■　　■

The following book review was published in *Field & Stream*. It was written by Ed Zern. Attend!

Although written many years ago, *Lady Chatterley's Lover* has just been re-issued by Grove Press, and this fictional account of the day-by-day life of an English gamekeeper is still of considerable interest to outdoor-minded readers, as it contains many passages on pheasant raising, the apprehending of poachers, ways to control vermin, and other chores and duties of the professional gamekeeper.

Unfortunately, one is obliged to wade through many passages of extraneous material in order to discover and savor those highlights on the management of a Midlands shooting estate and, in this reviewer's opinion, this book cannot take the place of J. R. Miller's *Practical Gamekeeping*.

This little girl was nervous about getting her haircut in a barbershop, so the barber gave her a lollipop and talked to her soothingly and all was going well. Halfway through, however, he noticed something amiss.

"Hey," he said to the little girl, "you're getting hair on your lollipop!"

"Yes," she said cheerfully, "and I'm only eight years old."

Anyboy like to hear a shaggy ass story? Oh, all right. Don't *clamor!*

This bemused gentleman walked into a saloon and asked for a whisky and water. The bartender said, "Tickle my ass with a feather." The customer felt that this response was not quite what he had expected.

"Whad you say?" he asked. The bartender smiled and responded: "I said, 'Strictly nice weather.'"

The gentleman (he may have been the traditional Englishman) had his drink and then walked a bit and came to another saloon. He entered and stood at the bar.

"What'll it be?" asked the bartender.

"Oh, nothing really, just poke a feather up your ass."

The bartender felt that his response was not quite what *he* had suspected and said, "Huh?"

And the gentleman said: "Rather cool out, isn't it?"

Here is a literary joke, meaning that it has some ignorance in it. Pronunciation ignorance. I was once at a literary party and a well-known humorist said to me: "How would you like to collaborate with me on a science-fiction novel?" I said, "Well, maybe." He said, "It would be set on Uranus during a big war among the planets. We could title it, 'Up, Uranus!'" I gave the matter some grave thought, and finally I told him, "Sounds like a fine idea. I'll work with you on the book provided you agree that we'll do a sequel, to be titled, 'The Wiping Out of Uranus.'" He said he would, and we didn't.

■   ■

Hard-drinking men have told me that the most violent trauma connected with their guzzling is the phenomenon which they call, with little affection, the shakin' drink.

A man gets up with a ferocious hangover and no dog-hair in the pantry. The whibbies are upon him with such intensity that he is certain to die flopping around on the floor in great agony if he does not get a couple of drinks real soon. So he throws on some clothes and heads for the nearest saloon.

The bartender brings him his double whisky, serving it perhaps in an old-fashioned glass at the request of the customer. Now comes the nerve-rending moment of truth. There may be only one or two other drinkers in the place, and they are attending strictly to their own affairs. Yet our man has a feeling that every eye is upon him. He knows that if he picks up that glass of whisky, it will begin to shake in his hand the moment it leaves the bar. It will shake with increasing rapidity if he attempts to move it toward his face. If he persists in his determination to get that glass to his mouth, the shaking will become so violent that he will likely spill every drop of the whisky, slopping it all over himself. If he were in a room alone, he would be able to make it, but something in the psychology of the situation makes him feel other eyes upon him, critical eyes, scornful eyes.

In the folklore of boozing there are accounts of how men with the shakes have used the bar-towel as a sort of lever, the rag being placed around the neck and the drink being *drawn upward* to the face, the left hand pulling on one end of the towel, the right hand grasping the other end, and the drink, at one and the same time.

The big drinkers say this solution is pure poppycockery. It can result, in mid-action, in a violent nervous upheaval and complete mental collapse. There are stories, too, of the sick one carrying a soda straw with him, but that is no good—the true solution would be one that does away with all chance of embarrassment before other people.

And so for centuries the problem went unsolved until one morning when Rodge Starr of the old *World-Telegram* walked into the Greenwich Tavern, dying on his feet. He ordered his double and then followed the procedure of all such ailing men—he stood and looked at it, and looked at it, and looked at it. He *had* to have that drink, but there were two other men down the bar, and there was Louie the bartender, and Rodge *knew* they were all staring at him. He'd glance at them, and their faces would be turned away, but they weren't fooling him. They were watching him slyly, the damn sneaks!

Rodge must either struggle that drink up to his face, no matter how much shaking, no matter how much spilled en route, or he must turn on his heel and walk out of the place. No more violent an inner debate ever raged in a man than that one. He would move his hand slowly toward the glass, and there would be no apparent shaking, but he was well aware of the fact that the instant he took a grip on it, the shaking would start. And so he stood, suffering mightily, and then something spoke to him, his guardian angel, or a creature from outer space. Like a shimmering, iridescent ray from the blue this great inspiration came to him.

"Hey, Louie," he called out to the bartender, and as Louie turned toward him, he asked, "What ever happened to that crazy son of a bitch used to come in here took a drink like this?" And he took it—shakes and all.

■   ■

A gentleman who was twenty pounds overweight took himself to a health farm where, a friend had told him, they really stripped off the pounds. They told him the course came in three sessions. He could take the first, which cost twenty-five dollars;

then he could take the second, which was fifty dollars; and if he wanted it, he could take the final session for a hundred dollars.

He decided to try Number One. He was told to strip. He was then led to a small field beside a forest. Out of the woods came a bewitching girl, naked, and carrying a poster which said: "If you can catch me, you can aroint me." He took out after her and ran himself ragged for about an hour and never caught her, but when they weighed him there had been a nice loss of suet.

The next day he came for Session Two. Same procedure. This time a redheaded sexpot came out of the woods. She was more beautiful than yesterday's blonde, and she seemed listless. Kinda tired. Her sign said: "If you can catch me, you can aroint me." He made a dash for her, and ran her up and down and around the forest for an hour, and never laid a hand on her. A substantial reduction in weight.

Now he decided on the full and final treatment. The third day he stripped and was taken to the small field. Out of the woods came a grizzly bear. A sign hung round his neck, saying: "If I catch you, I'm gonna aroint you!"

That day our boy didn't even stop to get weighed.

■   ■

A neatly dressed man, an accountant, called on the madame of a well-established whorehouse. He said that it was imperative that she get him a woman at least six feet tall and weighing less than ninety pounds.

The madame figured, well, she had seen all kinds of wierd-ohs in her time. She rather enjoyed new things and here was something with the sound of novelty. Still, the guy was a kook, so she said she'd take care of the matter and he went away and she dismissed it from her mind.

A week later the accountant phoned and said that money was no object. He said he'd pay up to three hundred bucks for just five minutes with such a scarecrow. He said it was important to the even tenor of his existence.

The cited sum aroused the madame's true interest. A few days later on a streetcar she spotted the tallest and skinniest woman she'd ever seen, a drawn-out Vogue model with an ugly face to match. The madame approached this bundle of slats and made the proposition and the skinny one, never propositioned in her entire life, agreed to do whatever was required for fifty dollars. So it was arranged and the madame made a date with the eager accountant.

He showed up at the appointed hour, accompanied by a beautiful little girl of the *early* Shirley Temple type. The little girl was holding his hand tightly, and the madame was mildly horrified, and wondered what on earth kind of a perversion this bird had in his mind. Then she shrugged. A deal is a deal. She advised the guy that the woman was a little *over* six feet and a little *under* ninety pounds, but he just grinned broadly, and said, "Oh that's good! That's *real* good!" And she thought to herself, my God I'd kinda like to *watch* this one! She collected the money and directed the guy to the room at the top of the stairs.

He took the sweet little girl by the hand again and mounted the steps and arriving in the room found the living skeleton waiting.

"Take off your clothes," he ordered, and she took them off, and stood before them in all her grotesque angularity.

The man now turned to the little girl and in a soft voice said: "Now. You see what happens if you don't drink your milk?"

■   ■

I still feel that the greatest and most succinct commentary on gambling came from the typewriter of Damon Runyon.

The old gambler knew he was dying, and he felt that he should give his son and heir some profound advice before proceeding to the Great Las Vegas in The Sky, and when the lad arrived at his bedside, he said:

"Son, as you go around and about the world, some day you will come upon a man who will lay down in front of you a new deck of cards with the seal unbroken, and that man will offer to bet you he can make the jack of spades jump out of the deck and squirt cider in your ear. Son, do not bet that man, because just as sure as you do, you are going to get an earful of cider."

■   ■

I took a personal buffeting when that 1938 hurricane hit the New York City area, raging across Long Island and whamming into New England, much to the surprise of all concerned. Yet the main reason I remember the storm is the story that came out of it.

A dirty-rich gentleman living in the Hamptons out on Long Island was in Abercrombie & Fitch's big Manhattan store early that August and after picking up some special fishing tackle, bought himself a handsome new barometer. He took it home and hung it on the wall in his big house. A few days later he gave it a glance, and was startled. He took it down from the wall and wrapped it up, enclosing a note to Abercrombie & Fitch, saying:

"This instrument is defective. At 11 a.m. this date it registered *hurricane*. Please send me a replacement."

He got in his car and drove to the nearest postoffice to send off the package, and when he got home . . . his house was gone.

■   ■

Gracie Allen once remarked, rather offhandedly, that her grandfather was slightly eccentric. "Sometimes," she said, "he would put a paper bag over his head and go around saying, 'Where *is* everybody?'"

■   ■

There was a party on Nob Hill in San Francisco during which the engagement of a beautiful young lady of quality and a splendid defensive tackle would be announced.

In the course of the party much champagne was consumed and shortly before the moment when the announcement was to be made, a young fellow who had been belting away at the grape called the football player off to one side.

"Don't marry her," he said. "You'll be making a big mistake if you do. I've known her for years. She's been scrozzled by every able-bodied man and boy on Nob Hill."

The defensive tackle reflected on this statement for a moment, then smiled tolerantly.

"Please!" he protested. "It's really not a very *big* hill."

■　■

Variety carried a dispatch out of Moscow in 1967 concerning a documentary film on the career of Isaak Itkind, a Russian sculptor just turning 95. In the course of the picture Itkind said he did not want to die, because the fact that he was an artist would likely mean that he would go to Hell. And he did not want to go to Hell, because he suffers from a bad case of asthma, and it is his understanding that in Hell there is a great deal of cooking —a steady, ceaseless broiling of sinners—and this would create a lot of smoke, and smoke would be bad for him, and he would have to spend the rest of eternity coughing.

Makes sense.

■　■

Jim Thornton was one of the great wits of American vaudeville, a monologist with a true talent for the ad lib, a composer of bright songs, and a drinking man of scope. Joe Laurie, Jr., the historian of vaudeville, said that there were more legends surrounding the boozing of Jim Thornton than around any other person in the annals of show business.

On one occasion Thornton and another monologist, George C. Davis, embarked upon an extended bender and at the end of two weeks they were broke . . . and hideously thirsty. Jim Thornton was a man who could stay drunk for months and still keep himself shaved and washed and his clothes pressed. His friend Davis, however, grew more slovenly and dirty with each passing day of a brannigan, and now, after two weeks of carousing, he looked a fright. He was filthy.

Being desperate for drinkin' funds, they walked together along Broadway until Thornton spotted another vaudevillian and approached him and asked for the loan of two bucks. The man inspected the two monologists and shook his head. "Make it *one* dollar," begged Jim. "Nope," said his friend. "Then how about a *quarter?*" The friend almost shouted his *no*.

"Is that final?" asked Jim Thornton.

"That's final," said the friend.

Thornton drew himself up in all his dignity, assumed an imperious air, turned slowly to the unkempt George Davis, and said: "George, *throw a louse on him!*"

■　▧

A charter member of The Brotherhood was Ed Penisten, and the only member thus far to take his departure. Ed Penisten, whose true name was Ed Penisten, died in Chillecothe, Ohio, his native town, in 1965. He was a retired sportswriter, and once served as sports editor of the Columbus *Dispatch*. He wrote to me often, sending me dozens of fine earthy Midwestern tales, and his letters sparkled with Rabelaisian wit. In one of his notes he said:

"After an illness I asked my doctor if he thought I was ready for a mild sort of sexual intercourse and he said, 'Hell, there ain't no such thing.'"

Ed composed the following piece, which he could recite very effectively at stag dinners and in the locker rooms of golf clubs— he knew all the important golfers of his time. He was rather proud of *Dowagiac* because, as he told me, "it is a description of a very delicate affair without the use of a single off-color word." I'm happy to present it as:

RECITATION NO. 11

Dowagiac

One day back in the Prohibition era I was leaving my room at the Deshler in Columbus and I almost collided with a distinguished-looking old gentleman of the type that Thomas Nelson Page has made us love so well—the Old Virginia Colonel. I recognized him as a friend of many years standing and knew that I had something that he would enjoy. I said: "Colonel, come to my room, sir. I think I have something that will interest you."

In the room I opened my grip and pulled out a bottle of prime Bourbon whisky and handed it to him. The old man fondled the bottle for a moment and I told him to help himself.

He said: "Thank you, Ed, I don't mind if I do. I been up to Dowagiac on a mos' tryin' trip fo' the pas' two weeks and yo' invitation is really the act of a Good Samaritan. It is, indeed." The Colonel had himself a couple of stout pulls, and then he cleared his throat, and began:

You know, Ed, it's gettin' to be a hell of a state of affairs in this land of ours, with a bunch of prohibitionists tryin' to force water down our throats. As Bobby Burns once said, "Man's inhumanity to man makes countless thousands mourn." My Mama raised me up on the Bible and I've read it through from Genesis to Revelations, and the only place in that Great Word, sir, where a man called for water, was a man that was in Hell, sir, where he belonged.

Now, Ed, you know I'm a hossman. My father befo' me was a hossman, and his father befo' him. I know a likely lookin' filly when I see one. You know that, Ed.

Well, sir, as I was passin' through Detroit, on my way up to Dowagiac, where I always winter my hosses, I was walkin' down Dearborn Street when my eye fell on a filly that was easy on the eye. A kind of golden sorrel, she was, with a pair of eyes that were soft and yet challengin'. The look that John Taintor Foote has called "The look of eagles." The look of a thoroughbred, sir.

Well, as I stood there admirin' her points she turned and looked me square in the eye and before I knew it, Ed, my hat was off and we were talkin' together like old friends. And finally she says to me, "Colonel, you goin' to be in Detroit for long?" And I says, "No, ma'am. I'm ketchin' the fo'-twenty over the Michigan Central up to Kalamazoo to meet my stable boy Jody and then I'm goin' on up to Dowagiac, ma'am, where I always winter my hosses." And she says to me, "Colonel, why don't you take me along?" And I says, "Why, ma'am, I'd be delighted."

So we ketch the fo-twenty over the Michigan Central to Kalamazoo and go down to the hotel and I buy her some candy, and magazines, and knick-knacks, and I say to her, "Honey, you go on up to yo' room. I'm goin' to stay downstairs and talk to Jody 'bout the hosses fo' a while, and then I'll be up to see you."

Well, I stay down there talkin' to Jody 'bout the hosses fo' a half hour or so and then I go up to her room and knock on the door and she says, "Come in." I open the door and she's standin' there without even a blanket on her, sir.

Now, Ed, you know I'm a hossman, but here is the likeliest-lookin' filly I ever see. Not a blemish on her, from her fetlock to her mane. Full-rounded withers, deep in the chest, so sound that if you was to just tap her, sir, she'd ring like a bell.

It didn't take me but a few seconds to peel down to my racin' silks and I laid her on the bed and stepped into the saddle fo' a trial heat.

She started to spring out from under me like as if I'd socked the spurs to her, but you know I'm a hossman, and a judge of pace. Didn't let her have her head. Just kept holdin' her under wraps and pattin' her on the neck and sayin', "Steady gal! Steady!"

We reach the quarter and she's runnin' like a machine, me settin' easy in the saddle, just ridin' high and breezin' her along.

We reach the half, and she's goin' strong. Hadn't drawed a long breath, Ed. Didn't have to urge her none. Never had to lay the bat on her. Fact is, I was just hand-ridin' her.

We reach the three-quarters and she starts fightin' fo' her head. But I just kept holdin' her steady. And then I started to ease her off a bit, gettin' ready to shake her out and start her spring fo' the wire.

Then we turn into the stretch and when the wire was in sight I kind of push out on the reins and say, "Go baby! Go fo' home!" Ed, she damn near th'owed me clean out of the saddle!

And then I rode 'er from there. I took her home. We come down that stretch with the dus' a-flyin' and just workin' together like a fine machine. I was ridin' her with knees, heels, elbows and hands, sir. And just befo' we hit that wire I called out to her, "Hit it, baby!" And we jumped fo' that wire like we was jumpin' fo' Heaven.

Now, Ed, you know I'm a hossman from way back, and I gave her the finest ride I ever gave a filly in my life. But just after we pass under the wire and was just a-layin' there pantin' and sweatin', I be doggone if she don't look up into my eyes and say to me:

"Colonel, sir, I been layin' here a-wonderin'. How do you all *spell* Dowagiac?"

TALES TO AMUSE
A TURNED-ON SOROPTIMIST

It is a matter of remark among professional vulgarians, such as myself, that many women are clearly inconsistent in their reaction to certain unrefined situations. It has long been well known that a girl will exhibit herself on a beach in a bikini, showing enough meat to feed the hands on the King Ranch for three days, but that if a gust of wind should whip up her skirts on a city street, exposing her thighs to public view, she might very readily give forth shrieks and whinnies of embarrassment.

This state of affairs may be changing with the bewildering changes in fashion lately, but the idea still appears to be valid. I'm acquainted with a college-bred lady who holds an important editorial post on a national magazine and who, one might suppose, would be inclined toward broad-mindedness. She *is*. But in things that she reads, not things that she hears. Unless (and this is important) she hears them in the legitimate theater. She has long been a steady customer of mine and has read something over twenty of my books. Those books, for the most part, are deliciously vulgar with a liberal use of four-letter words; some people have even classified them, to my great delight, as obscene. This lady editor has never said a single word to indicate that anything in any of my books offends her.

Recently I was in her office and I tossed a little gag at her, asking her if she knew how a Dutch housewife measures butter.

"She smears it on a plank," I said, "and slides down the plank, and what sticks to her ass is a pound and a quarter."

A loud exclamation of protest! I was ordered to leave her office! She behaved as if I had tried to commit an assault upon her! And I have not had a word out of her since!

■   ■

Henry McLemore, the Georgia redhead who assisted me in bringing on the Depression of the 1930s, plus various tidal waves and volcanic disorders, World War II, and the corn earworm blight of 1929, tells one of the best Ring Lardner stories. Henry says he got it straight from Grantland Rice.

Rice and Lardner had a hotel suite together in Chicago where they had been covering an important sports event. Lardner had only a weekly column to do whereas Rice was turning out daily pieces. When Lardner was in the clear, he laid in a supply of Old Whipping Post. He sat down in an easy chair, facing a wall on which there was an old English sporting print showing two jumpers coming over the last barrier in the Grand National.

For two days Lardner sat in that chair, gazing steadily at the print, taking a drink occasionally, going to the bathroom, eating a sandwich, but always staring at the picture. Grantland Rice came and went, and brought in friends, but Lardner never stirred from his chair, never stopped looking at the wall.

"Finally," said Rice, "the day came for us to pack and go back to New York. Ring was still in the chair. I packed. I discovered that he was already packed. I called the bellhop to come for our bags. After he arrived in the room, Ring got out of the chair and we all started through the door toward the elevators."

Lardner suddenly turned and walked back into the room and took a final look at the picture on the wall. Then, at last, he spoke to his old friend:

"Granny, the jock on that second horse isn't trying."

■ ■

From time to time some individual in the literary world will give forth a list of what he considers to be the ten most beautiful words in the English language: *azure, moonlight, tranquil, melody, shadow, golden lullaby,* and so on. The list of one man seldom agrees with the list of others, but the newspapers for some reason always enjoy printing these things.

Ring Lardner was once going through his newspaper when he came upon such a list. He read it through, slowly, pronouncing each word carefully as though testing its beauty. At the end he raised his eyes and asked: "What's wrong with *gangrene?*"

■ ■

On a wintry day a kindly matron stopped in a pet shop to nuzzle puppies and talk baby-talk to kittens and coo at birds. She happened to notice a pretty little rabbit and decided to buy it and take it to some neighbor children. On her way home she slipped on the icy sidewalk and fell heavily. In the fall the rabbit was killed and the matron, being a tender-hearted person, was so upset that she burst into tears, while still down on the concrete.

A gentleman who may have been drinking came along at this moment and taking note of the lady's weeping, and of the creature lying dead at her side, felt the urge to comfort her somehow.

"Don't cry, madam," he said. "It would have been an idiot anyway. Look at the ears on it."

■ ■

Two suburban ladies who were neighbors were having mid-morning coffee.

"Myra," said Nancy, "you always seem to have such wonderful clothes, from the good stores, and I can't get my husband to kick in with any money at all for such things. You got some kind of special technique you use on Ed?"

"In a way, I have," said Myra. "It used to be that Ed wouldn't let me buy anything nice at all. He said housedresses were all I needed most of the time and housedresses I got. One morning

174

while he was still in bed I walked into the room stark naked with my shopping bag in my hand. He opened his eyes and looked at me a few minutes and then asked me where I was going. I said I was on my way to the supermarket. He said, 'Like that?' I said, 'Like this.' I added that, since he refused to give me money for decent clothes, this was the way I was going to do my shopping from now on. He got right out of bed and kissed me and rubbed my bottom and said he was sorry and then went and got fifty dollars out of his wallet and told me to go buy myself a nice dress. From that day on he always gives me money for nice clothes without a bit of argument. Why don't you try it on Walt, Nancy?"

Nancy did. A few mornings later she entered the bedroom while Walt was still asleep. She was naked and had her shopping bag. He opened his eyes and looked at her and said, "Where the hell do you think *you're* going?"

"Shopping, at the supermarket."

He stared at her another moment.

"Well," he growled, "you might at *least* shave."

And turned over and went back to sleep.

■ ■

Wilson Mizner was one of the greatest *destructive* wits this country has ever produced, and destructive wits are the best kind. He spent his later years in Hollywood where, I believe, he had some kind of ownership connection with the Brown Derby restaurant. He is the man who, on his deathbed, came out of a coma to find a priest saying prayers over him. "Go away," said Mizner, "I've been talking to your boss."

At one of the big movie studios—let us call it Mammoth Pictures—a press agent one day came up with a fine idea and took it to the head of the company. "This Mizner," he said, "is a great character, always being quoted in the columns. Why not hire him as a writer for Mammoth? It wouldn't make any difference if he didn't write anything. We'd get the studio a lot of publicity just by having him under contract."

And so it was done, and right away a stag dinner for columnists and studio heads was arranged to announce the hiring of Mizner. He was never known to have turned down money under any circumstances, and he had of course accepted the job.

At the dinner there were several speeches in which glowing tribute was paid to Mizner, and much was made of the coup by which Mammoth Pictures had acquired his services, and then the great man himself was called upon for a few words. He stood up and let his eye rove over his audience and then spoke:

"Working for Mammoth Pictures," he said, "is like banging a porcupine—it's a thousand pricks against one."

■ ■

At the country club in Morganton there was one member who made a practice of taunting fellow golfers with: "I got a gorilla at home that could beat you at this game."

One afternoon in the clubhouse he told one of the club's best golfers that his gorilla could beat thim, and there was a flare of temper.

"I wish," said the golfing star, "you'd shut up about your God damn gorilla. I'm gettin' sick and tard of it."

"He still could beat you."

It now came out that the man actually *had* a gorilla at home and that the gorilla knew how to play golf and the argument reached the point where a bet was made—that on the following morning the gorilla would play the man eighteen holes for a $100 bet.

At the appointed hour the human golfer was ready at the first tee and the gorilla's owner arrived with his monster in a station wagon. Ground rules were established and it was agreed that the gorilla should drive first. He stepped onto the tee and with no preliminary fiddle-faddle, using an extremely unorthodox stance, he swung. The ball shot straight and true—four hundred and fifty yards to the rim of the green.

His opponent promptly flung up his hands in despair, and exclaimed, "Oh my God! How can you expect a man to beat that kind of idiot golf? I give up! I surrender! We don't have to take another step. Here's your hundred bucks."

So the gorilla was led back to the station wagon and all hands went indoors for a round of drinks, and during these no-hard-feelings ceremonies, the loser said:

"I needn't say that no golf ball was ever hit harder, farther or straighter. But I was just wondering—how does your boy putt?"

"Same as he drives. Wham! Zoooom! Four hundred and fifty yards!"

■　■

The vice president of an important corporation was hauled away for surgery and a day or two later a most heartening note was delivered to him. It said:

"The board of directors wish you a minimum of discomfort and a speedy recovery by a vote of five to four."

■　■

Back in the times when the wowsers of our land were concentrating their fire against such birth-control advocates as Mrs. Margaret Sanger and Dr. Marie Stopes, and warring on anything that popped up with the look of free love, a leader in the crusade was a certain New York clergyman of wide celebrity, a grim, unsmiling Protestant churchman who stood high in the hierarchy. One day he submitted himself to a press conference and George Britt, who was present, told me later of a thing that happened there. Bishop Gordon (not his name) was saying that most women were actually in favor of abstention from sex. Pressed on this subject, he said that most women don't care a fig for it and wouldn't mind passing it up altogether. George Britt spoke up.

"How do you know this to be true, Bishop Gordon?" he asked. Said the Bishop: "Mrs. Gordon told me."

■　■

A correspondent in a southern city has written:

"The other day Freddie Coates and I were having a bit of

revelry down at the club, shooting a little gin rummy and belting away at a bottle on the table. Along came the local Methodist minister and stopped at the table and took in the situation and then began lecturing us on our behavior. Freddie listened until the preacher finished, then faced him and said: 'Now *you* listen, you meddling, bible-thumping, pompous old fart. If you don't stop yammering and poking your nasty nose into my business I'm going to be forced to say something to you that you might not like.'"

■   ■

Willie Collier was one of the greatest comedians ever to grace the American stage. The day after he died in the 1940s I was in Beverly Hills and ran into Gene Fowler, who had been a warm friend of the old actor. Gene said that Collier died with family and friends at his bedside and that his parting words were a trifle offbeat. Aware that he was dying, Collier looked around at the people in the room and then said, "Don't anyone tell Jessel."

■   ■

During the Hitler War I had an interesting letter from an American soldier in the Philippines. This soldier had read several of my books that had been distributed in "Armed Service Editions" around the world and he felt that I was the man to answer a question that was bothering him. He wrote:

"I wonder if you would be able to tell me what part of a woman is her yet. We have been puzzled about it out here in the Philippines. We know that a woman has got a yet. The reason we know it is that we heard an officer talking the other day. He said there was a girl in Manila who had been shot recently and the bullet was in her yet. Please tell us what it is."

I wasn't able to oblige the boys right away. But I took the matter of a woman's yet to my literary agent. He is a man who knows everything and he wasn't stopped by this one.

"Yes," he said, after a few moments of reflection, "I know what a woman's yet is. It's the same as her now."

"And what is her now?"

"Oh, you know," he said. "Don't you remember? I wonder who's kissing her now?"

I wrote of these scholarly confusions some years back and subsequently a letter came from a reader in Australia. He told me of a story in a Sydney newspaper about a man who was happily married for thirty-eight years and then one day his wife vanished and, according to the newspaper, "he never saw her more." The gentleman who wrote me said that maybe that was the reason she disappeared. Of course I still don't know what is indicated, what all this means, no more than I know what is meant in the story of the lady who fell heavily on the sidewalk and the fall seriously bruised her somewhat.

■ ■

I seldom drive past one of those baskets without remembering the time when . . .

Bob Cousy, one of the greatest basketball players of the game's history, was riding down the thruways from Boston with several friends, headed for New York City. They came to a toll-gate and Cousy steered into a passage equipped with metal basket. Employing his vaunted grace and dexterity, he tossed his quarter. And missed.

■ ■

Scrap of dialogue overheard in a London club:

"I say, Frothing-um, did you hear the news of old Blenkinsop?"

"Old Blenkinsop? Thought he was in Inja."

"He is. The latest word is, he's left Lady Blenkinsop and gone to live with an ape."

"An ape? Old Blenkinsop? Gad! Fawncy that! Tell me, Dugdale, is it a . . . er . . . a female ape?"

"Of course, man! Nothing queer about old Blenkinsop!"

■ ■

An American businessman came up with a bad toothache while visiting in Mexico City. He made a try for a couple of *norteamericano* dentists but they were out playing golf or at the races. So the manager of his hotel gave him the name of a Mexican dentist with an office close by, and the gentleman got an immediate appointment.

From the first he was apprehensive about the technical capabilities of a Mexican dentist and, in fact, of any Mexican and, in fact, of any foreigner anywhere in the world. His misgivings increased when he saw that the Mexican dentist *looked* like a Mexican and so he said, as politely as he could, that he'd like to ask a couple of questions. Certainly, said the dentist. Had he, the dentist, ever worked on the teeth of an American before? Oh, *si, senor.* Had he ever worked on the teeth of an American *businessman* before? The dentist thought for a moment and then remembered one New York businessman he had served.

"I'd like to have his name, and telephone him before we go any further, if you don't mind," said the nervous Gringo. "I'm sure you'll understand." Of course, said the dentist, and got the name and number.

The tourist returned to his hotel and in half an hour or so had the New York businessman on the phone. He identified himself and then said:

"Did you ever have your teeth worked on by a dentist named Garza in Mexico City?"

"Yes, I did," said the man in New York. "About two years ago."

"What sort of a job did he do for you?"

"Let me tell you," said the New York man, "that yesterday I was on the golf course and on the seventh hole my drive was short and hooked into the rough. I was out there poking around, looking for the ball, and a fellow on the tee didn't notice me, and he drove, and his ball came straight at me like a rifle shot, just as I was turning around, and it hit me right in the balls, and I want to tell you that was the first time in two years that I haven't felt my teeth hurting me."

■　　■

A couple of old coon-hunters were sitting on the front porch of the postoffice in Mallmayzon, Arkansas, and as was their custom took to lying about the talents of huntin' dogs they had owned. The winning story for the day:

"I had a yeller hound oncet, smarter'n manys a human, used to send him out by hisself to get the coons. Way I'd work it, I'd whittle out a piece of board the shape of a coon-hide stretcher so he'd know the size I wanted him to fetch back. I'd set the board out against that tree in my back yard and that yeller dog he'd look at it and go get me a coon to fit it. Sad to say, I lost that wonderful smart dog. One mornin', two year ago, my old womern spilt some wotter on her arnin' board and took it outdoors to dry and set it against that three and, 'y God, my yeller dog ain't come back *yet*."

■　■

Young Paisley Forbush had a great yen for the theater. He loved everything about the drama and he wanted most of all to be an actor. His ambition did not falter after his parents were killed in a plane crash, leaving him several million dollars. He still yearned to be an actor, to play *Hamlet*.

Money will buy almost everything and in this case it was necessary for Paisley Forbush to buy his way onto the stage. Rebuffed everywhere else (though they happily took his money for their Broadway productions) he finally set up his own company, hired actors and technicians, and produced his own *Hamlet* with himself, of course, in the starring role. The show was mounted with style and no expense was spared. Mr. Forbush even persuaded some critics to attend the opening night.

From the first curtain it became apparent that this was to be a shambles and a farce. Paisley Forbush had been unable to engage any actors of repute; the ones who responded to his golden call were as hammy as he. And never in history had there been such a job of hamming as Paisley gave to the role of Hamlet.

After a while the audience decided to have fun. There were critical remarks from the orchestra, and then jeers, and then boos, and from time to time concerted hissing. Then the audience began to throw things. Articles of clothing and even shoes and finally fruit and vegetables rained on the actors. They, however, moved relentlessly forward with their play.

Came the time for the soliloquy, and Paisley Forbush was just getting well into it in spite of the hail of objects from across the footlights. Then someone threw a seat cushion—a seat cushion with metal springs in it. The heavy cushion struck Hamlet full in the face, stopping the flow of words.

Paisley Forbush stood for a moment blinking his eyes, and he placed a hand to his face to see if blood had been drawn. Then he squared around and faced the audience and cried out imploringly:

"Hey! Wait a minute, for Christ's sake! Take it easy! I didn't *write* this shit!"

■　　■

Bob Burns speaking again:

I remember the time we had the big blizzard down home. Snow piled up to the second-story windows. Everybody was marooned in their homes. Uncle Fud was lookin' out the second-story window of his store. There wasn't nothin' but a sea of snow as fur as the eye could reach. Not a sign of life. Suddenly on top of the hill, where Main Street dips down to Lick Skillet, he saw snow a-flyin' up in the air. It kept gettin' closer and closer. On down the middle of Main Street come this flurry of snow flyin' every which way.

Finally it was right under Uncle Fud's window and he could lean out and see what it was. It was a little old man with long whiskers that had been shovelin' a trench through that deep snow. My uncle says, "Where in the world did *you* come from?" The little old man says, "I dug my way here from fourteen mile back in the mountains." So Uncle Fud says, "You musta been desperate to dig your way fourteen mile through this blizzard." And the little old man says, "I'll say I was desperate. We bin outa nutmeg for six days."

■　　■

There is something cheery and nostalgic and sentimental to me in an obituary. My very first job of professional writing was that of composing death notices for an Indiana newspaper, and ever since then I have had a tender interest in obits. On that Indiana paper every obit was composed in the same form, and might have been stamped out by a machine. That may be the reason why I enjoy the account of the death and burial of John Rector.

Mr. Rector was the surveyor who laid out the town of McLeansboro, Illinois, where I was born. I found an account of his death in a history of Illinois, written by someone who had verve and imagination and style. Here it is:

> John Rector died May 25, 1805, at the section corner of Sections 21, 22, 23 and 28; buried from this corner, south 62 degrees west 72 poles, small stone monument, stone quarry northwest 150 yards.

In the files of the McLeansboro *Times* for 1907 I came across a column of school news. One item said that Tom Barker had pulled a girl's hair in school whereupon the teacher told him he had to write a composition of fifty words. Tom Barker sat down at his desk and (I swear I didn't make this up) wrote the following:

> Jessie was fond of kittens. She saw one in the road and called, "Here pussy, pussy."

I know of no Thomas Barker in American literature, yet surely that boy grew up to become a writer of consequence. Perhaps he's in advertising.

■ ■

    Two well-dressed, middle-aged women had been commuting from Cambridge in to Boston every Friday morning, usually in the same car, often side-by-side in the same seat, for a dozen years. In all that time they had never spoken. Then one day

Mrs. Z. said: "My dear, we have been taking this trip together for so long, I think it would be all right if we talked to each other now, don't you?"

"Yes, indeed," said Mrs. B. "I was just thinking the same thing. I have a husband who is quite old. He can't get the things he wants, he isn't able to do the things he'd like to do for me. He has grown quite feeble, and so I go to Boston every Friday to get scrod."

"Imagine that!" said Mrs. Z. "A real coincidence. My husband is in the same condition and can't do a thing for me. So I go in to Boston once a week for the same reason. But this is the first time I've ever heard it spoken of in the past tense."

■ ■

Doug and Ed met at the office water cooler one morning. "I had a blind date last night," said Doug. "Man, oh man!"

"How'd she turn out?" Ed asked.

"Who?"

"The girl."

"There wasn't any girl. I had a date with Willie Trumpkin and we went out and got blind. Man!"

■ ■

Wanna know who made that blind-date joke up? I did. Right on the spur of the moment. Here's another hand-wrought non-dilly.

The cop has a roughneck prisoner under the blazing floodlight in the back room of the stationhouse.

Wham! A blow to the face with the truncheon.

Whop! A bust in the snoot from the cop's fist.

Now the prisoner speaks: "Hey Mac, fuh cry sakes go a little slow! If it wasn't fuh guys like me, guys like you wouldn't have no job!"

■ ■

And just to prove my versatility, I add a spoonerism of my own invention. Most spoonerisms are spoken by accident. I say

184

this from my exalted position as one of the nation's 986 foremost authorities on spoonerisms. This one was devised in the interests of delicacy. It is a reproach: don't be so stucking fuffy!

■ ■

Sam Lapidus and his wife, being prosperous, decided to send their daughter to Europe where, they felt, she might find a rich husband and at the same time acquire some cultural interests.

After a few weeks Penelope, the daughter, wrote and asked that a good book of etiquette be airmailed to her.

Her parents were pleased. "Real fine people she's mitting," said Sam, and shipped off the book. A couple of months after that and there came a request for another book of etiquette.

"Ah," beamed Sam. "Princes and dukes and oils she's dating," and sent her Amy Vanderbilt.

At the end of two years Penelope arrived home with a baby in her arms.

"Whose baby is?" Sam asked.

"Mine."

"And the papa?"

"I don't know."

Sam stared at his daughter in astonished anger, and then cried out: "Two books on etiquette you got and you don't even know how to ask, 'With whom am I having the pleasure?' "

■ ■

Farmer Jackson was plowing the northwest ten of his south forty when he noticed his teen-aged daughter Myrtle, a backward girl who had never even seen a real guitar, running toward him from the direction of the house.

"Maw's havin' a spell!" cried Myrt when she reached her father. "I think she's dyin', Paw! Hurry!"

Together they galloped for the house and arriving there found Maw spread out on the floor, but she was now stirring, and she opened her eyes, and shook her head briskly, and got to her feet and said, "Pshaw an' shuckin's, I'm all right, sound as a dollar, git on with yore plowin'." So her husband returned to the field.

A week later little Myrt came kiting across the clods again, with the same dire news, and Farmer Jackson ran all the way to the house just in time to see Maw struggling to her feet and returning to her churnin'.

A third time it happened, and little Myrt told her Paw that it looked like the end for sure, but Maw came out of it and went right to work stirrin' the apple butter.

The fourth time, Farmer Jackson still couldn't slow his pace, but ran every step of the way, and in the house he found Maw again on the floor, lying still and white. He leaned down and flicked up an eyelid, and then felt for her pulse. None.

"Well, naow," he said. "*That's* more like it!"

■　　■

The late Buddy DeSylva, when he was head of production at Paramount and, for a time the current Boy Wonder of Hollywood, hired a New York book writer who had just produced a humorous best seller. The author told Mr. DeSylva at the beginning that he knew nothing about the dramatic form, that he didn't think he could ever turn out an original screenplay.

Mr. DeSylva suggested that he employ the old tried-and-true formula, something about (1), let the boy meet the girl; (2), get the boy out on a limb; (3) saw off the limb, and (4), something else I can't remember.

The New York author disappeared into the Writers' Building and a few days later sent a memo to Mr. DeSylva. He said that he had been unable to do anything with the formula that had been suggested. Instead, he had devised a formula of his own, and he asked Mr. DeSylva if he thought it workable. This is the way it went:

1. Let the boy meet the girl.
2. Get the girl in a pickle.
3. Get the pickle in the girl.

Mr. DeSylva responded, interofficewise: "Your formula shall prevail in the studio from now on. A new day has dawned. Let us all now proceed to make millions."

This is a true story.

I know.

I was there.

RECITATION NO. 12

February, 1963.

Bulletin for The Brotherhood:

Most of you are aware of the discovery I made several years back of Lawrence Welk's way with the word "heart." Mr. Welk has a Dakota-Teutonic accent which will not permit him to enunciate a terminal "T." With him a terminal "T" becomes a "D." It was in February of 1957 that I first heard Mr. Welk presiding over a Valentine's Day show on television. The program consisted exclusively of songs with the word "heart" in the title and Mr. Welk personally introduced each number.

To the best of my recollection the songs his people sang and played included these:

YOU BELONG TO MY HARD.

MY HARD TELLS ME.

HARD ACHES.

BE CAREFUL, IT'S MY HARD.

MY HARD STOOD STILL.

I LEFT MY HARD IN HONOLULU.

SO BEATS MY HARD FOR YOU.

ALL OF A SUDDEN MY HARD SINGS.

THE MANSION OF ACHING HARDS.

PEG O' MY HARD.

ZING, WENT THE STRINGS OF MY HARD,

and
THE CURSE OF AN ACHING HARD.

So yesterday I noted in *TV Guide* that Mr. Welk would be doing Valentine songs again, and last night I had him tuned in, and he started right off with this merry announcement:

"Tonight we are going to salood both Valentine's Day and Hard Month." And they did.

He brought out the girl who plays the ricky-tick piano and said she was going to play "Hard of My Hard" and she really soared with it. He introduced one singer as "a boy who puts his hard in his work" and the boy obliged with a vigorous rendition of "You Gotta Have Hard."

Soon after that Lornce introduced his Irish tenor. "Here's a young man," said the Dakota maestro, "with a big voice and a hard to match." His song was the tender, "Yours Is My Hard Alone."

I recommend that members of The Brotherhood jot it down on their calendars for next February. Just in case somebody doesn't believe me.

BUSKIN' UPSIDE DOWN
OVER UTAH

I have for your delectation this evening a rare item from the private papers of Gene Fowler. If I seem to dwell overmuch on the exploits of Fowler, it is because I enjoyed his friendship and I considered him to be a genius in many directions, not including music. He was dead set against all Hawaiian music and for this baffling heresy I sometimes think that it'll be a month of light-years before he struggles out of Purgatory with a scorched butt.

Gene's son Will is an adequately salacious contributing member of The Brotherhood and has his Paw's lusty attitude toward life. Will Fowler, if I may speak metaphorically, doesn't own a decent bone in his body and wouldn't know what to do with such a bone if he had it.

One of the most interesting personal things I know about Gene Fowler is contained in the writings of his friend Ben Hecht. On a hot summer evening Fowler was occupying a room at the Hotel Algonquin in New York. He was standing naked in the bathroom, brushing his teeth, when the water glass slipped from his hand, hit the edge of the basin, broke in pieces, and one fragment struck him viciously in the peter and lacerated same.

The wound was bleeding so profusely that Fowler put in a hurry-call for his friend Dr. Sam Hershfeld, who sped to the Algonquin and went to work with needle and cat gut. During this procedure, it is said, Fowler ignored Dr. Hershfeld's urgings that he relax and keep quiet. He kept up a loud and endless torrent of cursing and wailing and moaning, all to the effect that his love-life had been destroyed forever and that he had nothing to live for and that Dr. Hershfeld should please put him out of his misery. The howling of the patient was so unnerving to the doctor that in sewing up the wound he made a long seam of baseball stitches. A baseball stitch is used to make two edges meet precisely, and according to the Big Webster, is "worked under and over from the inside outward." It is commonly employed on the covers of baseballs and in mending tears in sails. It would seem reasonable to assume that this was the first time it was ever used on a peter. In after years Fowler was proud of his stitches and said they gave him a quality that other men lacked, though he admitted that he sometimes grew nervous whenever he was around baseball pitchers.

What's that, Miss? You don't think I should come right out and use the word *peter?* What would you have me say? Member? Oh no, my dear—*you* are a member. I thought you told me that you were educated in a convent and knew all. Well, if the word offends you, I'll make a change. I remember once being in the home of Jimmie Street in Chapel Hill. Jimmie was talking about a novel he was writing at the moment, a novel about the voyage of Columbus, and he was telling stories he had turned up in his research. One of these anecdotes had to do with Columbus's peter, and Jimmie remarked that he was not going to call it a peter in the book.

"What I'm gonna use," he said, "is the Spanish for peter—I don't know it right now but I'm gonna look it up."

A lady who was present said: "It's *Pedro.*"

So, my dear, henceforward I will employ the Spanish term if that would suit you better. I will always say that Gene Fowler had baseball stitches in his Pedro.

Now.

One of Gene Fowler's finest books is *A Solo in Tom-Toms,* which is a wild and glorious account of his youth. Soon after it

190

was published in 1946 I had a letter from him. In it he made a passing reference to a book he had just read which gave him "the best time I've had since coming into manhood." That expression in turn led Mr. Fowler into a most remarkable bit of self-revelation. He said that he had cut one small episode out of the manuscript of A Solo in Tom-Toms and he passed the cut portion along to me. Now his widow Agnes—the only woman ever good enough and salty enough to have been the wife of Gene Fowler—has given me permission to publish, for the first time, the story that was removed from the book, and I'll call it . . .

SEX AND THE SAWMILL

By Gene Fowler

Several magnificent books have been created in our time by men who stood naked in their inkwells. As against these works, there appear a profusion of monologues that rely for their celebrity upon grim apostrophes to the physical routines. The matter of the glandular debut becomes the golden text of these brooding raconteurs. They see themselves as the actual discoverers of practices commonly known to young males, and rabbinically denounced as long ago as the time of Onan, one of the five sons of Judah.

There is an amazing sameness of pattern to be found in memoirs that emphasize the first apple: the seduction by the governess, if the author be an aristocrat; or by Nasty Nellie the village slut, when the writer is of thatched-roof antecedents. There are slight variations in theme, to be sure: the boy lured to the house of ill-fame, or initiated after school by the teacher; or introduced to the *et ceteras* of barnyard and alley.

To relieve modern letters from a tedium of design I shall touch upon the time it "happened" to me in my fifteenth year, and at the sawmill of the McPhee & McGinnity Lumber Company, where I now worked on Saturdays. One of my duties at the lumber yards was to stand the other side of old Cal Ullery at the tail-end of a slotted bed upon which planks were ripped to size by the zinging buzz-saw. The sawyer was

Mr. Maybee, a man with the face of a hippogryph and the methodical temperament of a kappelmeister; part of one thumb and all of his sense of humor were missing. He fed the new boards by twos, fours, or sixes, to the shining-toothed wheel. Cal and I received and then stacked them.

On the day of my brisk elation, there were no fair faces or shapely bodies to be descried among the piles of sawdust or the pyramids of boards. As I stood braced to receive the crawling, vibrating planks, an unexpected impulse caused me to leave abruptly the vicinity of Mr. Maybee, his helper, and the noisy saw. Mr. Maybee did not view my desertion of the boards as a pardonable action; nor did he approve of old Cal's diabolic merriment.

I never pass a pine tree without tipping my hat; I may have known its mother.

■   ■

There are certain stories in which the cast of characters changes with, almost, every telling. For example: A high-toned British lady, sitting next to Winston Churchill at dinner, grew so exasperated with his remarks that she finally exclaimed, "If I were your wife I'd put poison in your coffee." To which Sir Winston replied: "Madam, if I were your husband, I'd take it."

That story has been written and told, to my own knowledge, about Franklin D. Roosevelt and Clare Boothe Luce, Errol Flynn and Mary Pickford, Richard Nixon and Tallulah Bankhead, Bill Veek and Alice Roosevelt Longworth, Gary Cooper and Ilka Chase, and Mickey Rooney and Elsa Maxwell. The first time I ever encountered it, the insults were exchanged by Dizzy Dean and a lady in the grandstand.

Now hear this: One hot afternoon back in the 1920s Dorothy Parker rang the doorbell at the apartment of George S. Kaufman. Inside Mr. Kaufman had been sitting around naked. He was expecting the arrival of Moss Hart at any moment and the two were going to work a few hours on a script. Mr. Kaufman answered the doorbell, still in the nude. He and Miss Parker stood looking at each other in silence for a long moment, then Miss Parker said in a cool and queenly manner: "Don't look now, George, but I think your fly's open."

I have heard that story at least fifty times and in every case the cast of characters changed. A quarter of a century ago in Hollywood Charles Brackett assured me that Jed Harris was the naked man and Ina Claire the lady with the queenly cool.

Among the other performers who have been cast in this bit of Broadway folklore are John Barrymore and Tallulah Bankhead, Jackie Gleason and Carol Burnett, Alexander Woollcott and Pola Negri, Harold Ross and Beatrice Lillie, George Jean Nathan and Marilyn Miller, James J. Walker and Tallulah Bankhead, and Billy Rose and Anita Loos. The loveliest-seeming couple appearing in the charade were Rudy Vallee and Edna May Oliver. Though the fellow who told me about it couldn't recall for certain whether it was Edna May Oliver or Zasu Pitts.

■　■

More about two of the theatrical ladies mentioned above. At 4 o'clock one morning Tallulah Bankhead and Beatrice Lillie arrived in the lobby of the Savoy Hotel in London. They had been attending a party and they were somewhat unsteady on their feet. Equilibrium was shot to hell, especially in the case of Miss Lillie, whose proper title was Lady Peel. She was in a sleepy condition. Somewhat out. She was residing, temporarily, in a suite at the Savoy and this was the destination Miss Bankhead had in mind as she summoned her strength, put on an air of great dignity, kept a firm grip on Miss Lillie, and spoke to the desk man: "Lady Keel's Pee." The clerk gawped. "I beg your pardon?" he said. And Tallulah repeated, firmly: "Lady Keel's Pee!" The man still didn't understand and began to stammer, whereupon Miss Lillie came out of the fog just long enough to wobble her head around and exclaim imperiously: "You heard 'er, *my pee!*"

■　■

In the Boston Pantheon as viewed by Cleveland Amory one of the most vivid personalities is Helen Choate Bell. Her quips were many and memorable and Mr. Amory calls her, without qualification, Boston's greatest talker. It was Mrs. Bell who declared, in an age when Henry Ford was a tongue-tied bantling, that the automobile was destined to divide mankind into two classes: the quick and the dead.

My own favorite story about this grande dame is concerned with her dislike of vegetation. Other society women of Boston joined garden clubs and coddled flowers and whooped it up for Arbor Day, but never Helen Choate Bell. She once said to a friend who was leaving for a day in the fields and forests, "Kick a tree for me." It came about, from time to time, that Mrs. Bell did find herself in rural surroundings and on one such occasion a field of asparagus came in view. She asked her friends what it was and when they told her, she approached for a closer view.

"Hm-m-m-m-m," she mused. "And I always thought cook braided the ends in the kitchen."

■   ■

Two male patients, attended by a female nurse, were sitting on a bench on the lawn of a mental hospital. A large bird, possibly an osprey, was flying over the grounds and in passing let go an untidy deposit on the bald head of one of the patients.

The nurse, fearing the sullied lunatic might throw a conniption, cried out excitedly, "Don't move, Herman! Stay right on that bench! I'll be back in three seconds with some toilet paper!" Whereupon she raced off toward the nearest building.

Herman sat a few moments without moving, then turned his head slowly and said to the other patient: "She must of lost her mind. That bird'll be forty miles from here by the time she gets back with that paper."

■   ■

I think it was Pat O'Brien who spoke of a fellow-Catholic who was so devout that he blessed himself and spoke a few words of grace before biting off a hangnail.

Mr. O'Brien enjoyed remembering the Father Murphy of his

194

boyhood in Milwaukee. One Saturday night Father Murphy was hearing confessions at Gesu church. He had been through a trying day and now it seemed that everyone in the parish was turning up for confession. Father Murphy listened to a few and then peeped through at the many who were waiting. It was a hot night and he was bone-tired and sweating. At last he stepped out of the confessional and spoke to the crowd:

"All ye mortals stay, and all ye venials go home!"

In two minutes the church was empty.

■   ■

    Mrs. Pfsorzimer noted that her husband was in low spirits when he arrived home from the brewery where he had worked as bookkeeper for twenty-two years. She asked him if anything was wrong.

"Wrong!" he exclaimed. "Nothing's wrong, only that the boss fired me half an hour ago!"

"Fired you! What on earth for?"

"Just because I misspelled a word," said Mr. Pfsorzimer. "I misspelled one little word in a letter I sent to the bank."

"What was the word?"

"Firkin."

She stared at him in disbelief for a few moments. "*Misspelled* it!" she then exclaimed. "Why, you dumb jerk, you don't even know how to *pronounce* it!"

■   ■

    The Vice-Prisidint of our land, said Mister Dooley, hangs rather low in the firmament. "Ye can't be sint to jail f'r it," he went on, "but it's a kind iv a disgrace. It's like writin' anonymous letters . . . Some Vice-Prisidints have been so anxious f'r th' Prisidint's safety that they've had to be warned off th' White House grounds."

Following his election to the Vice-Presidency, Hubert H. Humphrey announced that he had done a bit of digging into the history of the high office he now held. His findings stirred him to the very marrow. "Who can forget those storied Vice-Presidents of the past?" he cried. "William A. Wheeler! Daniel D. Tompkins! Garret A. Hobart! and Henry Wilson!"

■   ■

A pretty young thing who worked as a stenographer in a London barrister's office came home one evening and told her mother she was in the family way.

"Who is the man?" demanded Mums.

"My boss," said the girl.

Mums barged into the barrister's office next morning and read several riot acts and said, "What are you going to do?"

"I will see that your daughter has the best of everything," he replied. "She will go to a good hospital and have the finest doctors. If the baby is a boy, I will set up a fifty thousand pound trust fund for him. If it is a girl, twenty-five thousand. I don't like girls."

"And," said Mums, "if it is a miscarriage, can she have another chance?"

■   ■

A town I enjoy visiting in Southern Mexico, when I can get the dough together for the long trip, is Oaxaca. Among my friends there is Paul Perez, a retired Hollywood screenwriter and a raconteur of rare capabilities and charm. I believe I have spoken of Paul before.

Recently he wrote to me about a village Plume Dance held by the Indians in his area. During the fiesta a young man of the village approached a Gringo tourist gentleman and said, "Senor, would you like to come see my seester?"

The Tourist said, "What for?"

"To make lawve to her, of course."

And the Gringo said, "My God, I don't even drink the water!"

■   ■

The late H. L. Davis, novelist and gentleman who once copped a Pulitzer Prize in fiction, lived his final years in Oaxaca and was a warm friend of Paul Perez. They spent many afternoons playing Scrabble on the veranda of the Davis house. During one of these games Paul put together the word "nookie." Harold Davis looked at it a long moment.

"Paul," he finally said, "I don't think you'll find that in the dictionary."

"At my age," said Paul, "I don't think I'll find it *anywhere.*"

■   ■

A dozen or more years ago there was an epidemic of so-called Shaggy Dog stories, and it has not subsided completely to this day. This type of story originated in London, according to people who are supposed to know about such things, and the first of the lot may have some historical interest. A man put an ad in the London newspapers saying he had lost a large shaggy dog and that he would pay a liberal reward for its return. Some days later he answered his doorbell to find a gentleman on the stoop with a large dog, quite shaggy.

"Did you advertise that you had lost a large shaggy dog?" the gentleman asked.

The other man took one look at the dog on the stoop.

"Not *that* shaggy," he said, and closed the door.

■   ■

Two men were talking at the check-in counter of Eastern Airlines at JFK.

"Last time I was here," said one, "my wife was with me and we were heading for a couple of weeks in Miami. I had a beautiful new set of matched luggage. Brand new. Well, right here at this counter we got into a fight. Screaming and yelling, and she being so God damn unreasonable and all, and finally I went out of my head completely. I had to hit her. I didn't wanna be *too* brutal and hit her with the big bag, the three-suiter. So I hit her three times with the one-suiter."

■   ■

Sam the hat salesman, a man with a good business head and a taste for high living, got settled into his hotel room, ordered up a bottle, and looked at "Search for Tomorrow" and "Love of Life" on television while hurling a good deal down the hatch. At length—to put it nicely—he began to grow restless, and his thoughts turned on womanhood, so he went downstairs and consulted with a bellhop.

He had the address on a slip of paper but somehow, perhaps because he was slightly fuddled, he made a wrong turn and found himself in a residential area. He located the correct number on a house and rang the doorbell. An attractive lady answered and Sam began discussing his needs, and how much he was willing to pay if he got what he wanted, and when the lady caught on to what he was saying, she cried out, "Hector!"

Hector, her husband, a man carrying about 250 pounds of muscle, arrived on the double and quickly beat the living hell out of Sam the hat salesman right there on the front porch, and then picked him up and flung him in a nice parabola clear to the far side of the street.

Sam struggled slowly to his feet, brushed off a bit of dirt, then turned and glared back at the two people on the porch.

"By God!" he called out, "you people sure got a lot to learn about running a whore house!"

■   ■

Goodman Ace, a reader of gossip columns for many years, saw in one such an item saying that the actress Shirley Jones "is having a baby." Ace sat down and wrote to the columnist: "What do you mean by that statement? I know what 'infanticipating' means, and I've learned the nature of a 'blessed event,' and 'heir-conditioned,' and 'stork-bound,' and 'anticipating a bundle from heaven.' But what exactly does 'having a baby' mean?"

■   ■

A salesman was stopping overnight in a small Oklahoma town and after a miserable dinner at the local hotel, he went out to the street and asked one of the citizens if there was a movie in the town. Nope. A bowling alley or pool hall? Nope.

"What is there a man can do for entertainment in the evening?" the salesman wanted to know.

"Well," drawled the native, "you can go down to the drugstore. They's a freshman home from college."

■　■

A resident of Maine named Leete True was once asked if he believed in baptism.

"God yes," said Leete. "I've seen it done."

■　■

A U. S. Army captain at Fort Bragg told me about the Chinese cook named Wong. Back around 1920 Wong reported aboard a naval ship as cook, not knowing that this particular vessel was famous for its hazing of all new arrivals.

Although he was subjected to a whole series of pranks, Wong never lost his poise and accepted his hazing with grace and good humor. At last his tormentors concluded that he was a worthy shipmate, and a committee called upon him with a little speech.

"Wong," they said, "we want you to know that we are happy to have you in our crew. You are a good shipmate and we want you to be our friend from now on."

Wong was not quite certain.

"You mean," he asked, "no more tie Wong's clothes in knots?"

"No, Wong."

"No more throw water on Wong when he asreep?"

"No indeed, Wong. No more will we tie your clothes in knots, no more will we pour water on you or put crabs in your hammock. We greet you as a full-fledged member of our crew."

Wong smiled.

"Hokay," he said. "No more Wong piss in coffee."

■　■

The late William Frawley, who closed out a long and distinguished acting career in television's "Lucy" show, always seemed to encounter the same panhandler whenever he was in the vicinity of Hollywood and Vine. This particular bum, more unkempt than most, made a practice of approaching Frawley and asking for coffee money, and Frawley always responded with a buck.

One afternoon they met and the actor asked the beggar what he *really* did with the money.

"Now, Mr. Frawley," said the panhandler, "you're a man of the world and you must know that I don't buy coffee with it. I spend it on whisky."

"At least you're honest," said Frawley, "so come on inside with me and I'll buy you a drink."

They stepped into the Brown Derby and settled into a booth. Frawley signaled the waiter and when he arrived at the table, ordered, "Two double scotch-and-sodas."

Said the bum: "Make mine the same."

■   ■

During the Jurassic period O. O. McIntyre was the top Broadway columnist and his jottings were syndicated across the land. One day at a postoffice Mr. McIntyre saw a woman enter a revolving door. (In those ancient times it seems that postoffices were the only buildings equipped with revolving doors; don't ask me why.) A man came along behind the woman and gave the door a hearty shove, catapulting her into the lobby of the building. A moment later she stood in towering anger, face to face with the offending party, and she cried out:

"Who do you push I am if a taxpayer is all I hope!"

Thus it happens to many of us. During critical moments we tend to lose control of the language. Ben Bernie, of fond memory, had a Polish trumpeter in his band who could blow like Berigan once he had learned a piece, but learning went very slow with him. He was particularly slow at one rehearsal and Bernie lost his patience and chewed his ass. Out. This in turn made the Pole mad. He flung his trumpet to the floor and jumped up and down on it till it looked like the back room in a plumber's shop. Then he ran up to The Old Maestro and shook his fist under his nose.

"You listen to me, Mr. Bernie!" he yelled. "Just because I'm a Pole you think you can kiss my ass? Well, you can go to hell, that's what you are, and I'm the guy who can do it!"

■　　■

One of the neatest press agent feats of all time, in my judgment, had to do with the hotel magnate J. Myer Schine and a racehorse. Unhappily I cannot remember the name of the public-relations counsellor who thought it up. He had been hired by Mr. Schine to publicize the Roney Plaza in Miami. So one day he had his idea; he went out to Tropical Park and after some shopping around located a broken-down horse whose owner was happy to get rid of him for a few dollars. The press agent now went through the formality of having the horse's name changed from whatever it was before to "Harvest Moon." His next step was to get J. Myer Schine to climb aboard the old horse and sit still in the saddle while a photographer snapped his picture. The press agent then released the photo to the newspapers with the caption: Schine on Harvest Moon.

■　　■

An aging bachelor named Ginsburg, proprietor of a nice business in New York's garment district, finally decided to take a vacation in Europe and booked passage on the French line's *Liberté*. He was assigned to a table-for-two in the ship's dining room.

When he arrived for his first meal he found a goateed Frenchman occupying the other chair at his table. The Frenchman leaped to his feet, bowed from the waist, and exclaimed, "*Bon appetit!*" The New Yorker hesitated a moment and then, in turn, bowed from the waist and responded, "Ginsburg!" That was the extent of their conversation. At the next meal, the Frenchman bowed and said "*Bon appetit!*" and Ginsburg bowed and said "Ginsburg!"

This went on for a couple of days and then Ginsburg, a little unsure of himself, mentioned the matter to another passenger and found out the truth. So, for the next meal, Ginsburg made a point of arriving first at the table. When the Frenchman came along, Ginsburg jumped up, bowed, and said, *"Bon appetit!"*

The Frenchman bowed in return and responded, "Ginsburg!"

■   ■

Victor Mature and Jim Backus were playing in a Roman spectacle at the Paramount studio. Both men were costumed as Roman warriors, with glittering tufted helmets and glistening breastplates and white flannel knee-length skirts.

Just before noon one day Mature said to Backus: "I've got to chase over to the Valley to sign a paper, so I'll skip lunch. Come on and ride over with me and we'll stop somewhere and tilt a couple."

They didn't have time to get out of their costumes and so, twenty minutes later, they entered a bar in Encino. They were the only customers. The bartender stared at them as if the men from Out Yonder had finally made it to Mean Old Earth. Mature asked for two highballs. The bartender didn't move a muscle, just stood there staring.

At last Mature spoke again. "What's the matter with you?" he demanded. "Don't you serve members of the Armed Forces?"

■   ■

Among the delights of my newspapering days was an acquaintanceship with Cornelia Otis Skinner. She told me once that she had been having some difficulty with her eyes, and someone had given her a book in which certain eye exercises were prescribed.

Miss Skinner took this book with her on a trip to California and was reading it in the club car of the Santa Fe Chief. She arrived at a passage describing an eye exercise in which the forefinger is employed. She followed the directions. She held up her right hand a couple of feet in front of her face with the palm turned outward and the index finger extended. The book said that she should now move the finger from side to side, looking at it, then looking past it on one side, then at it again, then past it on the other side, keeping it moving back and forth all the while. She continued this exercise for a while and then she saw a man sitting beyond her finger. He was staring at her, almost leering. She yanked her finger down, realizing that to all appearances she had been sitting there wagging it at the man just as if she had been admonishing him, in a coy sort of way . . . as though she had been saying to him, "Ah, you gay dog! I know what's on your mind! Naughty, naughty!"

Miss Skinner was so embarrassed that she retired quickly to her bedroom and stayed there the rest of the trip.

■ ■

Robert Benchley enjoyed telling about the time his mother went down to apply for a passport. The man told her to raise her right hand and then he recited: "Do you swear to defend the Constitution of the United States against all enemies, domestic and foreign?" Mrs. Benchley snapped her hand down.

"Do I have to?"

"If you want to get a passport, you do."

"Well," she said, "there are days when I wouldn't." And she took the oath.

■ ■

A man gets along in years and takes to thinking that if he knows anyone, he knows himself. Then he goes into a haberdashery and tries on a suit, and stands in front of the three-way mirrors. He is shocked, and he thinks, "Who in the name of God is *that?*"

It is said that this pain is spared the customer at Brooks Brothers. There *are* no mirrors in Brooks Brothers—they simply stand the customer facing another customer.

RECITATION NO. 13

Near San Francisco is a sanitarium devoted to the treatment of mental cases and in this asylum, some years ago, was a man named, oddly enough, Fox. He had been a patient for ten years and now it appeared that he was well once again. One day he was summoned before the governing board of the institution, and they told him they believed that he was now normal and that they wanted to send him back into the workaday world. As a matter of routine they asked him what he would do with himself once he was released, and he studied the matter briefly in his mind and then said:

"I'm goin' out and get me the biggest slingshot in the world, and come back here and shoot out every God damn window in this place."

They looked at one another and sighed and shook their heads and sent him back.

After the lapse of another year they called him in again and when they asked him about his plans, he repeated his earlier declaration, and once more he was returned to detention. Another hearing after another year with the same result, and then the governing board waited two years before calling him in. This time it was different. When they asked him what he had in mind for the future in the event they released him, he said:

"Well, gentlemen, there was a visitor here a few months ago, a man who owns a big warehouse in Oakland, and he told me that he would give me a nice job when I am released."

"Fine! Excellent!" exclaimed the governors.

"So," continued the patient, "I am going to accept his offer. It will be wonderful. I will save part of my salary and eventually I will buy myself an automobile, and sometimes in the evening I'll drive around the city and . . . gentlemen, I hope you'll understand this . . . there may come a time when I'll see a pretty girl walking along the street, and I'll ask her if she'd like to go driving with me. Really, gentlemen, I . . ."

"We understand perfectly, Mr. Fox," said one of the governors, beaming at the others. "Go on—tell us what you'd do next."

"Well, gentlemen, I'd take the young lady to a nice restaurant and after that perhaps to a show, and then we would go riding some more, and maybe we'd come to a nice park with trees and flowers and grass. And we'd get out of the car and walk in the park, through the trees, and after a while we'd sit down on the grass in some secluded spot and . . . oh, gentlemen, I can't really tell you what I'd . . ."

"Go right ahead, Mr. Fox, it's all right. We want to hear it."

"Well, gentlemen, I think maybe after a while I would kiss the young lady, and . . . and . . ."

"Proceed with it . . . it is perfectly normal. And what would you do next?"

"Thank you, gentlemen," said Mr. Fox. "And so, I would kiss her, and caress her, and—after all, gentlemen, remember that I've been here so long, so many years—so after a while I would slide my hand down to her leg, and . . . but I can't go on . . ."

The governors were twitching in their chairs and their eyes were somewhat popped and one of them almost cried out: "Go on! Go on! It's wonderful! Exactly what you *should* be doing!"

"Well," said Mr. Fox, "if I must go on . . . I'd caress the young lady some more, and she would soon be willing to let me do anything I wanted to, so I'd slip my hand up her thigh, and I'd take hold of her girdle gently, and slowly pull it down, and slide it along her beautiful smooth legs, and . . . and . . ."

"Yes! Yes! Go on!"

". . . and I'd get that girdle off of her, and run like Hell with it, and make me the biggest slingshot in the world and I'd come back here and shoot out every God damn window in the place!"

ENTERTAINMENTS
FOR THE HOOK SHOP

The emergence of Alaska as the largest State in the Union brought on an eruption of Texas-Alaska jokes that may never come to an end. Just last night I heard a colloquy on television in which a singer from Texas was asked just how he really felt about Alaska taking over the title. "You jest wait," he said, "till all that ice melts up there!"

One of the Texas vs. Alaska stories comes to me from a friend in Ohio—a State that seems to be loaded with hearty raconteurs.

A large Texas gentleman departed from the banks of the Pecos to seek his fortune in Alaska. He was a bluff and bibulous man and he couldn't understand why, after two weeks of effort, he still was not accepted by the men of the town he had chosen for his home. He bought his share of drinks, and slapped his share of backs, and laughed at all the barroom stories, but the boys simply wouldn't invite him all the way in. Finally he went to the bartender in his favorite hangout and asked some questions. The bartender told him that there was a certain ritual which a newcomer had to pass through before he was accepted—a sort of test he must pass. The Texan asked the nature of the rites, and the bartender recited three steps he would need to take.

First, he must sit down with a full quart of whisky and drink it down to the last drop without once leaving his chair. Second, he must go forth into the frozen wilderness and shoot a polar bear. Third, he must bang an Eskimo woman.

"Hell's farr," said the Texan. "Alla them is easy. Ah'll take th' bottle uh whisky right now."

He sat down in the saloon and in thirty minutes had polished off the quart. Then he stood up, grinned a Texas-size grin, hitched up his britches, and headed for the great outdoors. He was a little unsteady on his feet, but all hands agreed that he had the look of a determined man.

Toward evening the saloon doors swung open and the Texan stood there, still grinning, but his clothes were in tatters and he was bleeding from deep slashes on both his face and hands.

"Now," he said in a loud voice, bracing himself against the side of the door, "now . . . gimmy a gun an' show me this God damn Eskimo woman you want me to shoot!"

■   ■

I'm not going to bother you with such worn-out set pieces as James Whitcomb Riley's privy poem, or the catalog of postures at the urinal, or General Patton's Speech Before D-Day, or *Down in the Lehigh Valley* or "George Takes Up Golf" or the touching ballad called *Texas Love*. These things are either too well-known or too vulgar and you know me, I set a limit. People ship me these things and I stick them away in my files with little notes addressed from me to Posterity saying: "I didn't write this dirty thing." And sign it. But as I say, I keep the stuff around just in case some filthy-minded individuals turn up on my premises, as a lot of them do, and seek to be amused.

I do have a few things filed under "wholesome and cleanly" and these include a couple of letters that have become standards, but which you good people may not have heard about.

For some years the following "request for sick leave" has been popping up in various quarters of the globe. It has been sent to me from the Orient and from Quebec and from Central America. Jerome Beatty, Jr., was told that it originated with a bricklayer in Barbados. It goes:

Respected Sirs:

When I arrived at the building I found that the hurricane had knocked some bricks off the top, so I rigged up a beam with a pully at the top of the building and hoisted up two barrels of bricks.

When I had repaired the broken place there were a lot of bricks left over. I hoisted the empty barrel back up again and secured the line at the bottom and then went up and filled the barrel with the bricks. Then I went to the bottom to unfasten the line.

Unfortunately, the barrel of bricks was heavier than I was, and before I knew what was happening the barrel started down, and jerked me off the ground. I decided to hang onto the line, and halfway up I met the barrel coming down and received a severe blow on the head and shoulder. I then continued on my way to the top, banging my head against the beam and getting my fingers caught in the pully. When the barrel hit the ground it bursted its bottom, allowing the bricks to fall out. I was now heavier than the barrel and so started down again at high speed. Halfway down I met the barrel coming up and received severe injuries to my legs. When I hit the ground I landed on the pile of bricks getting several painful cuts from the sharp ends and corners. At this point I must have lost presence of mind because I let go the rope. The barrel then came down, giving me another heavy blow on the head and putting me in the hospital.

I respectfully request sick leave.

■　　■

And another one which has a slight Gaelic tinge:

County Donegal, Ireland.
Nov. 5, 19—.

Dear Michael:

Your welcome letter received and me and your Aunt Bridget thank you for the money you sent. We had seven Masses said for your grandfather and grandmother. God rest their souls.

You have gone high places in America. God bless you. I hope you will not be putting on airs and forgetting your native land.

Your cousin Hughie O'Toole was hung in Londonderry last week for killing a policeman. May God rest his soul and may God's curse be on Jimmy Rogers, the informer, and may he burn to a crisp in Hell, God forgive him.

Times are not as bad as they might be. The herring is back and nearly everyone takes heart in making ends meet and the price of fish is good. Thanks be to God.

We had a grand time at Pat Muldoon's wake. He was an old blatherskite and it looked good to see him stretched out with his big mouth closed. He is much better off dead even though he will burn till the Damned Place freezes over. He had too many friends among the Orangemen. God's curse on the lot of them and double it for Muldoon.

Bless your heart, Michael. I all but forgot to tell you about your Uncle Dinny. He still has the old spirit. He took a pot shot at a turncoat from the back of a hedge, but he had too much drink in him and he missed. God's curse be to the dirty drink.

I hope this letter finds you in health and may God keep reminding you to continue sending the money. Father O'Flaherty, who baptized you, has now grown feeble of mind and picks at the coverlets. He sends you his blessing. Nellie O'Brien, that smelly thing you used to go to school with, has gone bad and run off and married an Englishman. Let us all pray to God that she dies in childbirth.

May God take care of you and keep you from sudden death. Don't forget about the money.

Your devoted,
Brownie.

■ ■

As fine a coinage as the English language has undergone in this century was an utterance of a young reporter on the Denver *Post* back in the late 1920s. In my presence one morning he spoke of having seen a certain blonde girl, known to us all, late the night before and she looked as though she had been having a very tempestuous evening.

"Boy," said the reporter, "was she bed-raggled!"

■　　■

The handsome young painter suddenly put down his palette and brush, strode over to the nude model, flung her to the floor and worked his will of her. When she recovered her breath she said:

"I'll bet you do that to every one of your models."

"No," he assured her. "You are the first."

"How many models have you had?"

"Just four. A Peruvian vase, a rose, a banana . . . and you."

■　　■

Consider, if you please, this picture-book plantation house, with its white columns and juleps and darkies, and the handsome young man of the family, a dashing boy who was just beginning to sow his wild oats. His mother's colored maid, Muffy, was young and feisty and clearly a girl with more than a smidgen of white blood.

One afternoon the young man persuaded Muffy to go for a walk in the woods with him. They met at the edge of the forest and then walked together for quite a long distance until they came to a cool clearing, with soft grass and birds twittering. The boy took off his coat and hung it on the limb of a tree. Whereupon the girl said: "I wouldn' leave your coat there if I was you."

"Why not?" the young man wanted to know.

"We may not come back this way."

■　　■

It's still one of the best lit'ry stories of our time. Nabokov's novel *Lolita* had just been published and was being discussed at a table in a fashionable New York restaurant.

Present was a visiting Frenchman who had not heard of the book.

"This novel," he finally said, "what is it about?"

"The hero is a middle-aged man who falls in love with a twelve-year-old."

Said the Frenchman: "A twelve-year-old what?"

■　■

The gentleman asked the pretty salesgirl: "Do you keep stationery?"

"I do," she replied, "right up to the last minute. Then I just go *cuh-raazy!*"

■　■

Two old maid sisters lived quietly and primly in a small Southern town, and each had her own pedigreed cat. They were inclined to be nosey about the affairs of their neighbors, and as for the cats—the sisters were so proud of their bloodlines that they would never dream of having their pets associate, in a common way so to speak, with other cats. The two animals were never permitted out of the house.

Came the day when one of the sisters met a man who liked her. Soon they were married and off they went on their wedding trip to New York. The following day the other sister received a telegram from the bride in New York. It said:

"I don't care what you do with your cat but let my cat out."

■　■

Richard Bissell's father was visiting the novelist at his Connecticut plantation. The elder Bissell, a businessman of some consequence, happened to pick up a copy of *Swann's Way* by Marcel Proust. Idly he read his way through eight or ten pages. Then he put the book down firmly and said: "Smart alec!"

■　■

Christopher Columbus came ashore in the New World and walked up to a pair of Indians standing at the edge of the forest.

"*Como esta?*" Columbus greeted them.

"Oh God," said one Indian to the other. "There goes the neighborhood!"

■   ■

Here's another of Ernie Ford's stories right out of the Tennessee hills.

A boy named Zeph missed school for three days and when he finally showed up the teacher asked him why. "Because," he said, "my Paw sleeps nekkid." The teacher said she was not interested in how Zeph's father dressed for bed; she wanted to know why he had been absent for three days. "I tole you," said Zeph, "it was because my Paw sleeps nekkid." The teacher was mildly exasperated, but now she said, "So your father sleeps naked. What on earth does that have to do with your being out of school three days?"

Said Zeph: "It's this way, teacher. The other night it was hot and sticky and Paw went to bed nekkid like he always does in hot weather. Durn the night there was a ruction out at the chickenhouse and it woke Paw up. He jumped out of bed and grabbed up his double-barled shotgun and crep out of the house. Our ole hound dog Blue come out from under the house and follered along behind Paw, and they got to the chickenhouse, and Paw pushed the door open and poked his gun inside and just then Blue cold-nosed Paw in the bee-hime and the gun went off, both barls, and teacher I been pickin' chickens for three days."

■   ■

John and Sue Perkins were desperately eager to have a child but two years of marriage had gone by without success. Finally their doctor told them that they were probably making a psychological mistake in their approach to the problem—that they were trying too hard.

The doctor suggested that they undertake a new method; that they refrain from intercourse until the moment they both developed a strong and immediate urge for it. If the urge were powerful and simultaneous, then they might get a pregnancy.

A couple of months later they returned, beaming, for Sue was pregnant. They thanked the doctor and told him that they had followed his advice, and one evening the great urge had hit them both at the same time, while they were having dinner, and they had followed directions and . . .

"Well," said John, "it worked out perfectly, except for one thing. I don't think we'll ever be allowed in Howard Johnson's again."

■   ■

One of the classical jokes touching on the manner of speech which prevails in Brooklyn is the one about the boy walking in that borough's Prospect Park with his mama.

"Listen to that boid!" the child exclaimed.

"Not boid," corrected his mother. "It's a *bird*."

"Well," argued the kid, "it choips like a boid."

■   ■

A gentleman with a British look to him, horsey teeth glimmering in the California sunlight below a squarish black mustache, walked into a Los Angeles police station and announced that he wanted to report a lost camel.

"Camel?" said the lieutenant. "What kind of a camel?"

"Oh, just an ord'n-ry camel."

"Well," said the lieutenant, "we don't seem to have any report of a camel being found lately, so we'll have to have a complete description. Tell me, sir, does this camel of yours have any special distinguishing characteristics, birthmarks, deformities . . . anything of that nature?"

"Come to think of it," said the gentleman, "I believe he has a rawthuh large rectal orifice."

"Just what do you mean by that?"

"Well, yesterday I was riding him down one of your splendid freeways, and one of those *fraightful* little bug convertibles came up behind us, with two American fellows in it, and I heard one of them say to the other, 'Look at that big asshole on the camel!' "

■   ■

An organization of distillers was holding a dinner at a big hotel in Washington and in another room at the same time members of the Women's Christian Temperance Union were having a banquet.

In the hotel's kitchens someone made a mistake. The desserts intended for the distillers—watermelon soaked in brandy—were served to the temperance ladies while the booze people got plain ice cream.

The hotel banquet manager was soon aware of the mistake, but it was too late to make a change, so he held his tongue until both functions were over. Then he asked one of the waiters who had worked the WCTU banquet if any of the women had remarked on the watermelon.

"No," said the waiter, "I didn't hear any of the ladies say anything, but I did notice that quite a few of them were putting the seeds in their pocketbooks."

■   ■

Sherman Hoyt, a society yachtsman, was sailing a tiny sloop in a race to Bermuda. In mid-ocean he sighted the big liner *Monarch of Bermuda,* which had stopped for some minor repairs. Signal flags quickly appeared at the little sloop's masthead and the officers on the liner trained their glasses on them, to decipher the message. It said: "Can I be of any assistance?"

■   ■

As all of civilized humanity knows, the comedian Joe E. Lewis for years pursued a course of spending every dollar he made on booze and racehorses.

One day an acquaintance who was in the investment business called Joe aside, at a rare moment when the comedian was sober, and lectured him on the wisdom of frugality.

"All that money piling in on you," said the banker, "and you never save a cent of it. You've got to figure that some day the economic situation may change, and you should be prepared for it. You should start right now and put ten thousand dollars into a special fund, and then next year add another ten thousand, and keep at it for ten years, and then in case a big depression comes along, you'll have a nice nest egg of a hundred thousand dollars."

"Yeh," said Joe. "But suppose no depression comes along? Where does that leave me? Stuck with a hundred thousand dollars!"

■　■

An elderly lady entered one of those toney Fifth Avenue churches on a Sunday morning, carrying an old-fashioned ear trumpet so she'd be able to hear the sermon. She no more than got seated when an usher tiptoed over to her and whispered menacingly:

"One toot, and out you go."

■　■

The village wise guy came strolling past the blacksmith shop. He decided to watch the sparks fly for a while and stepped into the place. After a while he reached out and picked up a horseshoe. It was hot, and he let go of it real quickly.

"Burned you, didn't it?" grinned the blacksmith.

"Nope. It just don't take me long to look at a horseshoe."

■　■

An additional item out of the cultural pattern I acquired as a boy in the Midwest: A symphony orchestra from the East, led by an eminent conductor, was playing a concert in an Ohio city.

In the middle of a soft and sweet passage, the conductor suddenly swung his arms in a wild flourish, stopping the music. He turned and in a rage cried out:

"Who called that piccolo player a son of a bitch?"

215

A moment of silence, and then a voice from the gallery: "Who called the son of a bitch a *piccolo player?*"

■   ■

During a rehearsal at the Met, writes B. H. Haggin, the great Toscanini swore at the musicians and then said they "play like pigs." Members of the orchestra were sorely offended and demanded that Toscanini apologize, but he refused, and so they put down their instruments and left. Frenzied efforts were made to mediate the dispute but the Maestro would not give in. They play like pigs, he insisted, and he would not apologize for speaking the shining truth. At last he himself proposed a compromise. "Tomorrow," he said, "I go to rehearsal and smile and I say 'Good morning.'" And that worked.

■   ■

Bang the fieldpiece, twang the lyre! Ohio is checking in with another one.

An affluent gentleman was walking along Market Street in Akron when he noted the approach of a shabby and shambling character, quite obviously a panhandler. As the shabby man was asking the gentleman if he might have a dime for a cup of coffee, the gentleman stared at him intently and then said, "Aren't you Martin Busey?" The bum confessed it to be true, and hung his head. "Why," said the gentleman, "I remember you well from a year ago, and you were rolling in money, and as I recall you had all kinds of projects afoot. What on earth happened to you, that brought you to this sad condition?"

"Yes, Mr. Marberry," said the panhandler, "you remember aright. I will be glad to tell you, if you want to take the time to listen."

"Proceed, Busey, proceed, my good man." (I'm a son of a bitch if I ain't beginning to write like an English novelist. Crikey!)

The bum now related his tale: "When you knew me a year ago I was truly in the chips, Mr. Marberry. As a young man I had worked hard and saved my money and eventually I even

216

inherited a little. However, I was always fond of sporting events, especially harness-racing.

"One day I was out at the track when a young trotter caught my eye. He looked great to me, and when I found out later that he was for sale, I bought him. He turned out to be a fine investment. He won race after race and the money was piling in. Not long after that I purchased a pacer and this horse proved to be an even better investment than the first. There I was—the trotter was trotting and the pacer was pacing and the dough was just rolling in. Then came the night I was attending the fights and I ran into a manager who needed a fast few hundred and so I bought up the contract of a promising young club fighter. The kid turned out swell. In a few months he was fighting on TV and winning regularly and the dough keeps rolling in. I tell you, Mr. Marberry, it was peaches and cream! Meanwhile I had met a few boys who were involved in the rackets and somehow I wound up owning a house of ill-repute. That was *really* a goldmine. So this was the picture at about the time you and I met, Mr. Marberry: the trotter was trotting, the pacer was pacing, the fighter was fighting, the ill-reputers were ill-reputing, and I was getting richer by the hour."

"Good Lord," Mr. Marberry interrupted, "what possibly could have happened to upset such a lucrative group of enterprises?"

"I've nearly gone off my trolley trying to figure it out," said the bum. "All I know is that something happened and my trotter started pacing, my pacer started trotting, my fighter started ill-reputing and my ill-reputers started fighting and . . . please, Mr. Marberry, how about that dime for the cup of coffee?"

■　■

There was a time when Ernie Byfield's Pump Room at the Ambassador Hotel in Chicago was one of the great glamor restaurants of the nation. The joint, usually awash with celebrities and a required stop-over for movie people traveling coast to coast, was famous for its flaming meats, stuck on sabers and carried aloft from kitchen to table, spurting fire and smoke and hot juices along the way.

It is told that Jimmy Durante once escorted Martha Raye to dinner at the Pump Room. Miss Raye, enjoying her first visit to the celebrated restaurant, was studying her menu when suddenly, in the dimly lit room, an apparition appeared before the table—a waiter in glittering costume with a hunk of flaming meat on a saber. Miss Raye was startled and cried out in alarm as the waiter loped on down the room. Then she turned to her companion and exclaimed: "Whad he have on the enda that sword?" To which Mr. Durante replied, "Only a guy who left a dollar tip."

■　■

Mr. Byfield was once asked how he happened to get into the hotel business. He explained that his father had owned the old Sherman House in Chicago. "One afternoon," said Ernie, "he ran into me in the lobby, took a liking to me and put me to work."

■　■

An evil advertising man traveling alone through Pennsylvania stopped at a motel and during dinner in the little restaurant struck up a gay conversation with the lone waitress. She was good-looking, this waitress, and stacked, and whenever the evil advertising man said anything bordering on the vulgar, she pouted her disapproval.

The traveler brought forth his entire arsenal of trickeries and later, when the restaurant had closed down, the girl showed up in his room. She became coy and continued saying no-no-no and then he brought out the soft soap and finally he assured her that the thing he was proposing was endorsed and recommended by no less an authority than the Bible. This sold her, and she flopped over.

A bit later, she took to speculating, and finally she asked him if he was sure about what he had told her, concerning the Bible, and he went and got it, the Gideon version, and there it was in black and white, right inside the back cover: "THE WAITRESS IN THE DINING ROOM SCREWS."

■   ■

Several sideshow performers in a traveling circus were spending an off afternoon playing poker in one of the small tents. Their game was suddenly interrupted by a rustling of canvas and when they looked up, the show's biggest lion was standing before them. Cards and money and poker players went flying in all directions. When quiet was restored the man in charge of the box office was found cowering inside his wagon, still shaking with fright.

They brought him out into the sunlight and soothed him with reassuring talk and finally someone said:

"Calm down, now, Ferdie. That old lion don't have a tooth in his head."

"Listen," said Ferdie, "a lion can *gum* you to death!"

■   ■

An entire book might be compiled (and probably has been) with nothing in it but cracks spoken by drivers upon being stopped by motorcycle cops. Such as the one about the woman who was stopped for speeding and who said to the officer, "Well, if I was speeding so were you!" And the one attributed to Dizzy Dean on the occasion of his being interrupted while driving the wrong way on a one-way street.

"Couldn't you see," demanded the cop, "that this was a one-way street?"

"Sure I seen it," said Diz. "I'm only drivin' one way, ain't I?"

There are, too, certain sparkling responses made by the customers to desk clerks in hotels. A man without a reservation approached the desk in a Baltimore hotel and asked for a room. Nothing doing. Sold out. Filled up. Jammed.

"Ah, come on," he said to the clerk, "I know you always keep a few spare rooms."

"Haven't got a thing," insisted the clerk.

"Listen, pal," said the traveler. "Suppose President Johnson walked in here right now and asked for a room. You'd give him one, wouldn't you?"

"Certainly."

"Well," snapped the man, "he ain't comin', so *I'll* take it."

■　　■

Good friends, as we approach the conclusion of this season's seminars, I would like to serve up a little character study which I accumulated during visits to a certain town in the Midlands. Our subject: Bigger Budlong.

Bigger is the town's leading barber and is famous for many attainments, including a fine talent for cussing. He is now in his seventies and the last time I saw him his Basic English was still caustic enough to scorch furniture. He is bald and bowlegged and five foot ten. If his legs were straight he'd be well over six feet tall. He was a successful farmer in his younger days and played fiddle for the square dances, and even at his present age he loves nothing so much as getting into a good fist fight.

"I bin in a hundret and forty-one fights," he says, "and been whupped a hundret and forty-two times. One time a neighbor licked me twice durn one fight."

Thirty years ago Bigger Budlong's town was visited now and then by small circuses. These shows traveled across country by wagon and always included an elephant. It was customary for the elephant to go on foot from town to town and his progress through the countryside served to advertise the show.

In the time when Bigger Budlong lived on his farm, several miles up Shawbutt Crick, it was his custom to drive into town to do his barbering in the evenings and all day Saturday. On one particular Saturday morning he jockeyed his Model T touring car in from the farm and drove first to the mill to pick up some bran and middlings for his stock. He put the bags of feed into the back seat of his Ford, and then parked the car directly across the street from his barber shop.

Busy with his hair-cutting, he was all unaware of the arrival of the circus, with its elephant. The big animal came lumbering down the main street, paused beside Bigger Budlong's Ford, sniffed, and then walked straight to the car. He quickly located the sacks of bran and middlings, planted his feet firmly in the roadway and went to work with great snufflings and snorts and grunts of pleasure.

Bigger Budlong glanced up from his scissorwork and caught sight of an elephant lunching on fodder that was intended for the Budlong cattle. Bigger gave forth a profane yell, dropped his scissors and comb to the floor, and went charging into the street scattering dust and dogs and chickens and children before him. In his right hand he had a chunk of alum about the size of a tomato which he sometimes used to threaten disorderly customers in his shop. He stood now in the middle of the street, purpling the welkin with obscenities. Unhappily for American literature, there was no one present to take it down, but the witnesses said later that no more splendid cussing has ever been heard on this earth. Bigger rared back and let fly and the chunk of alum bounced off the elephant's hide as if it had been a peanut. It was noted that while Bigger's physical activity grew more frenzied with each passing moment, he actually moved no closer to the elephant than about, say, thirty feet. But finally he ran out of breath and paused a few moments, and glared at the elephant, and then, ready to renew his vocal assault, he took a tentative step nearer the foe, and spectators all along the street stood quiet so that a hush fell over the scene, and then Bigger yelled with all his might:

"You big two-tailed son of a bitch! If I knew which end your head was on I'd kick your God damned ass from here to Quincy!"

■ ■

And for our final curtain:

RECITATION NO. 14

Be it known that in the ancient Kingdom of Siam a most ingenious method was employed in the selection of a ruler. It was not only a marvelous system but, in a sense, a democratic one.

The old King died, and a new one had to be chosen. The first step was to dispatch Annamese scouts into every cranny of the kingdom in search of candidates. They sought, amongst nobles and peasants alike, the most virile and most handsome and best hung of all the young men in the land. Five of these stalwarts eventually became the candidates for the Throne, subject to a severe testing.

Now another contingent of scouts, from the Lawa and Yao Yin, went forth upon the land in search of the five most beautiful maidens amongst the populace—young women of stunning beauty, incredible shapeliness and untrammeled passion.

When the five young men and the five gorgeous girls had been chosen, the Great Day was announced. The Contest was held at midday in a great arena and the people of Siam gathered from far and wide to witness the ceremony. The moment had come for selection of the Lord of Life, Descendant of Buddha, Supreme Arbiter of the Ebb and Flow of the Tide, Brother of the Moon, Half-Brother of the Sun, Possessor of the Twenty-four Gilded Umbrellas, Spitter in the Golden Spittoon.

The five stoutly handsome young men lined up naked on the field. Twenty feet in front of them stood the five lovely young women, each naked and each carrying a brass pot filled with fine honey. When all was in readiness, the Royal Gakluk, clad in crimson *panung*, smote a mighty blow on the Sukhotai drum as a signal for commencement of the ceremony. Lesser timpani throbbed in the background as the five girls moved forward with graceful steps. Each took her position face-to-face with one of the young men, then dropped to her knees, and with her right hand took honey from the brass pot and began smearing it liberally, and caressingly, over the young man's lower abdomen; at the same time she employed her left hand in little pats and caresses of love. Five stout bowsprits stood forth for all to see.

When each candidate had been given an adequate coating of honey, sufficient to begin attracting swarms of large Siamese flies, the Sukhotai drum boomed once again and the girls stood up.

Another signal and each beauty marched around her young man, stood directly behind him, and then again dropped to her knees. Now each girl on signal reached through the sturdy legs and took hold of the proud bowsprit and, tugging with might and main, bent it downward and pulled it backward through the legs and then upward.

All was ready. The Royal Gakluk swung his great *klekti* against the drum, and each girl let go, and there were five simultaneous and lightning-like swishes as five bowsprits cracked against their owners' abdomens.

The one that killed the most flies—that was the new King.

Hence the name of the great capital city . . .

Bangkok.

■ ■

Now . . . throw money.

—END—